Variations on a Garden

Robin Lane Fox
Variations on a Garden

M

To my parents
whose garden is
full of my mistakes

SBN 333 17099 7

Picture Research by Louisa Lane Fox

First published 1974 by
Macmillan London Limited
London and Basingstoke
Associated companies in New York, Toronto,
Dublin, Melbourne, Johannesburg and Delhi

Printed in Great Britain by
Jolly & Barber Limited, Rugby

Contents

I went by the field of the slothful, and by the vineyard of the man void of understanding; and lo, it was all grown over with thorns, and nettles had covered the face thereof, and the stone wall thereof was broken down. Then I saw, and considered it well; I looked upon it, and received instruction.

Proverbs 24: vv 30-32

Among these people there is another water-hole of pure spring-water. In the early morning it is warm, but when the village fills at evening it is colder. In the middle of the day it is particularly cold, and that is the moment when they water their gardens.

Herodotus, IV. clxxxi

Introduction

If you ask what claims I have to know anything about plants, I reply that I began gardening at the age of nine and was fortunate to have parents with a garden of more than an acre and a long family interest in the subject. I spent my holidays gardening and I went to school first among a notable collection of rhododendrons, then within reach of the Savill Gardens at Windsor. When I was twelve I became interested in alpine plants, an interest which has grown better than they ever since. Other business has taken me to Greece, Turkey, parts of Iran and Afghanistan and the coastline inside the Arctic circle. I have tried to see as many wild flowers as possible though I do not find them easy to identify.

When I left school I went to the Botanical Gardens in Munich to work in their huge and unique Alpine Section. I owe much to the experience of their staff of seventy trained gardeners and to journeys with the Bavarian Botanical Society. I returned to go to Magdalen College, Oxford whose nearness to Oxford's Botanic Garden rescued me from an education without plants. Not until I was an undergraduate was I free, after ten years' confinement, to see my home garden and England's countryside in full flower in June.

Marriage caused me to rent a small cottage in the great gardens of Haseley Court, Oxfordshire, one of the finest designs to have been laid out since the war. I was extremely lucky. Many of these articles begin from my time there, and no gardener could fail to profit from the invention and excellent taste of Mrs C. G. Lancaster and her use of rare plants. In the years that followed, my time was occupied with writing a long book and practical gardening suffered. But I became interested in propagation, especially by seed, and I have raised more plants than I can now house. I have also enjoyed the chance of assisting with the three prize-winning gardens which the *Financial Times* have laid out at Chelsea Flower Show and I have been invited to arrange planting for gardens from the Scottish highlands to London backyards. The experience of gardening on many different soils has added much to a pleasure which has otherwise been centred on Oxfordshire, where my own garden occupies me.

This book has only come about because I have had many letters asking where it could be bought before it even existed. It derives from the articles which I have written weekly for the *Financial Times* since January 1970. I publish them because I have often been asked to; they will not teach you how to garden but I hope there may be plants and suggestions which will encourage you to garden more adventurously.

I have learnt from many gardeners and many books. *Everyday Gardening* by Mr Coutts of Kew first roused my interest, and the works of A. G. L. Hellyer, now my senior partner on the *Financial Times,* directed me more accurately than any since. Alice Coats's admirable *Flowers and Their Histories* has put me on the track of many surprising stories about plants, and Christopher Lloyd's *Well-Tempered Garden* has widened my view of a garden's scope;

though I still do not share his taste for brown foliage. This book, and my gardening, owes much to them all.

Lord Drogheda and Sir Gordon Newton gave me my chance to write about gardening and I will always be grateful for their boldness and encouragement. The present Editor of the *Financial Times,* and Mr W. W. Roger and Mrs Dorwald have seen to it that my weekly space continues to be filled. Their permission to reprint these articles and their tolerance of such unmonetary writings is one proof of my deep debt to them. Plants and finance are not an obvious pair, though the Japanese make banknotes from a shrub which is unusual for the way in which its twigs can be tied in knots.

January

Much is made nowadays of the merits of a garden for all seasons and this is a fashion which should be taken seriously. One flower in winter is worth ten in summer and we should all find a place for the winter irises, snowdrops and hellebores which keep the garden alive in the dead of the year.

The result is never a blaze of colour: a winter garden does not compete with a bright coalfire. Its pleasures are quiet, and none the worse for that. But they have to rise above their setting, and in January and February this can be very difficult. Between weeks of frosts and clear night skies, there is a mood in the garden which I describe as winter drip. Even a witch-hazel cannot shake it off.

This winter drip was very evident as I walked among the old stone walls of a college garden, praised by many for its summer display. Beads of rain hung on the bare stems of the shrub roses, while the earth beneath looked like a sodden brown carpet, not improved by groups of despondent ever-grey leaves. I know I like these plants, I told myself, but I do not want to live with them for the winter half of the year. As for evergreens, even they look wretched in cold weather. Being leafy, they drip more sadly than twigs and thorns.

I was wondering whether the whole garden would not look prettier in every season as a grass meadow, not a rose bed, when, tucked away in a southerly join of a library's wall, I saw a green-stemmed shrub with butter-yellow flowers. Doubts were dispelled like clouds in a brisk west wind. I knew no meadow would ever offer me the common winter jasmine and at once I was away in a world of fancy, far from weeds and yellow turf.

The bare-flowered jasmine, or *Jasminum nudiflorum,* is an unbelievably obliging shrub and like many obliging plants, its home is distant China. I like to see it sprawling in a tangle, not making its well-ordered way up wires on a wall. Most of all, in times of winter drip, I like it because of its family connections. It is a relation of the sweet, white summer jasmine which has never flowered very freely for me but has made up for its sparseness with a story which does the name of jasmine credit. The sight of its yellow-flowered winter relation turned my mind from dripping roses to a duke who once lived in Pisa.

Four hundred years ago, the jasmine grew in the Pisa garden of the Grand Duke of Tuscany. A cutting had reached Hampton Court but, for the purposes of the story, it had soon been lost by British incompetence: the Grand Duke was left with a monopoly of jasmine in Europe. Being as yet unacquainted with the doctrine of restrictive practice, he decided to keep his assets strictly to himself. Orders went out to the gardeners that not one sprig or flower of jasmine was ever to be given to a stranger: the punishment was five years' service in the sculleries. Most of the gardeners preferred their life with plants to the disgrace of a life with dishes and obeyed their master's instructions. Not so the superintendent of the ducal glasshouse. He might have been faithful if he had not loved.

Beyond the garden wall lived the penniless daughter of the Duchess's *femme de chambre*. She was adored by the glasshouse gardener who would give her a bouquet on her birthday, each year more special than the last. As time went by, each treasure of the greenhouse had been picked for her benefit and the gardener began to fear that next year he would be reduced to repetition, which might imply that his love was going stale. Only the jasmine remained to be given and, on the eve of the birthday bouquet, it burst into flower. The gardener could not resist it. First thing in the morning, before the routine watering, he picked a sprig for the lady he loved.

Never had his bouquet been more popular. She smelt it, and puzzled at the source of its curious scent; she wore it in her bodice and marvelled at its unfamiliar whiteness. Wishing to save its ingredients, she planted the pieces in a pot and six months later she found that only the jasmine was growing. When her next birthday came, the jasmine was in bud; quietly, she took more cuttings and two years later she had enough of a secret stock to start a stall of her own. The people of Pisa were entranced and such was the price they paid for her treasure that soon she could give her lover the present she knew he deserved. Twenty ducats from jasmine was enough in those days to start off a couple in a home of their own.

The Duchess, however, who had never cared for gardening, had been given a pot of stolen jasmine as a present from the Mayor. She wore it to dinner and the Grand Duke recognized it. Inquiry revealed the source; threats revealed its means of origin. But the Duke could not stand by his word. If he relegated his most skilled gardener to the scullery, the greenhouse would suffer, let alone the plates and dishes; meanwhile, his wife's favourite maid would hand in her notice and nobody would ever understand the problems of her powder case so well again. He gave in to the servants, and gardener and maid's daughter were married, as they wished.

The moral of this story is not that monopolies are mean or that even in Tuscany workers could break their employers' demands. It is only a story which adds to the jasmine's charm. There are flowers which have brought men together, just as they still take them out of themselves and their various preoccupations. They need attention and they also need knowing. But once known, they can roll away the gloom of the garden and by the faintest show of flowers, start off a train of fancy which leads very far from melancholy winter drip.

I well remember my first gardening dictionary: after a most elaborate chapter on how to pipe moraines, it drew up a complex plan of essential plants for the winter terrace. I doubt if any moraines are still bubbling, as even the most expert alpine gardeners now agree that rare alpines do not require those plugged basins of water to keep their roots wet. But though I used to ignore the winter terrace, I am beginning to think that given space, there would have been something in it after all. Witch-hazel, winter

Jasminum nudiflorum, Winter Jasmine. Arching and sprawling shrub; needs wire if it is to climb a wall unnaturally. Best to a height of 4 ft and width of 5 ft as a loose shrub. No pruning, except to save space. Flowers January–February. Increase easily by cuttings or outlying divisions from main clump: also by layers

sweet and winter iris are three plants I would like to enjoy in quantity in a separate winter corner. Space, however, is seldom available, and many of the prettiest winter-flowering plants demand room to spread in return for their inconspicuous flowers. The delight, of course, is to pick and smell them. But there is one winter plant which everybody can accommodate: I mean the highly sinister hellebore.

It is sinister because of its ancient properties. In the classical world, like the aconite, it was believed to be most poisonous. The Romans were agreed that it induced madness. In Roman comedies, when a slave might be about to discover that he was really his master's long lost brother, fathered from a matron now disguised as a music mistress (who was in fact his new girlfriend's identical twin) he would ignorantly threaten his next-of-kin with a dose of hellebore to heighten the drama further. Complicated plots did not first enter Italy with the rise of opera, but the hellebore, companion of stage intrigue, is the least complicated of garden plants.

We can all grow it because we all have a shaded corner, beneath a tree, perhaps, or against the back house-wall. The problem is to know which sort to choose, especially as hellebore names are an atrocious tangle. I am extremely fond of the common Christmas rose, *Helleborus niger,* but I have known it give great trouble and refuse to grow quickly. I do, however, urge you to try its shorter, whiter, larger-flowered variety called Potter's Wheel. This named variety is the finest Christmas rose and is far more conspicuous than ordinary seedlings. It is worth paying the price for it in order to be sure of the best. Apart from this favourite, there are two distinct kinds which I fancy.

The first is *olympicus,* the so-called black hellebore which was once believed to rejuvenate the aged. This monstrous claim is untrue but whether you are old or young it does not object to heavy shade provided that the soil is deep and rich. A very dry place beneath a tall tree would not suit it.

It flowers from January to March on stems about 18 inches high, though in the West Country I have seen it open by November. Its flowers are rounded; their greenish white fades to true green near their base and they hang their heads downwards, facing shyly into their broad evergreen leaves. They grow slowly from home-saved seed which ripens, if at all, in March. Though you have to be patient with your seedlings, it is well worth building up a colony.

The second is a plant I first saw in the wild in its native Corsica. My bus had a puncture on the way to the beach and while the wheel was changed, I made friends with *Helleborus corsicus* on a nearby hillside. I bless the iron spike that caused this delay: *corsicus* is an essential plant for any garden, not insistent on shade, whatever the books say, and much longer-lived in a stony soil. Its leaves are the best I know in the garden, except in March and April when the old growth is collapsing and the bronzed new growth has not yet replaced it. Shining, grey-green, pointed and

toothed, they grow into a very striking clump until they suddenly age and ask to be cut off, leaving the show to those fresh and thrusting young leaves. The flowers are apple-green, clustered in huge heads and they burst most abundantly from their fattened buds. Disregard the black fly they sometimes attract after flowering. They are well able to resist it.

Plants, however, are not immortal and *corsicus* may die when only five years old. It will almost certainly flop forwards and straggle before then. Enthusiasts are willing to stake it to keep it upright but this can look artificial. Mine are planted along the edge of a gravel path and though they fall forwards, they look appropriate as they break what would otherwise be a hard line. They also seed themselves happily into the gravel, which is now a nest of their seedlings. That, I feel, is the way to grow *corsicus* best, in a gritty soil as on a Corsican hill.

Though these two are my favourites, I urge you to try any spotted varieties you may find; they go by the name of *guttatus* and are seldom offered for sale. They are extremely pretty, especially when cut and closely inspected. Maroon spots mark their thick petals of cream or greenish white, making them the most beautiful winter flower in the garden. They are not cheap.

Cutting, however, brings me to the hellebore's one fussiness. The only way to make their flowers last is to slit the stems open for half their length and put them in warm water, renewing it each day. Do not use scalding water and do not slit the stems too high. *Corsicus,* however, is easier to keep, as you can pick each individual flower with a short stem and float it in a shallow bowl. It is pointless to pick the main stem as it is too thick for water to pass up to the flowers. These wilt within a day unless picked individually, but by floating them in a bowl you can enjoy them by the hundred, such is the crop of one plant of *corsicus.* Maybe we laugh at the luxury of the Edwardians' winter terrace, but with the help of the hellebore we can still move a mass of winter flowers indoors.

Winter flowers, like most others, have been improved by keen observers and collectors. We can all support this tradition, well instanced by the witch-hazel, whose yellow flowers and distinctive scent brighten January in many discriminating gardens. Our first plant was *Hamamelis virginiana,* discovered in a grove in Virginia some seventy years after the Mayflower first landed. Enterprising suppliers spread it around this country, yet one of its earliest reviewers curtly remarked that 'nothing more need be said to our people respecting this shrub, which Nature seems to have designed for the stricter eye of the botanist.' However, much has happened to the witch-hazel since 1742.

The last century was the great age of plant collecting in the Far East, and among the dangers of these expeditions, one important find was *Hamamelis japonica arborea,* the tall Japanese tree witch-hazel. It is not so tree-like in our climate, usually growing 8 or 9 feet high, but it bears its dark matt-yellow flowers from

Helleborus niger, Potters Wheel, large-flowered, short-stemmed Christmas Rose. Best in rich leafy soil in shade; 9 in high. Excellent form, found in a Staffordshire garden. Increase only by careful divisions in spring, but best left alone when possible

January onwards on the top half of the bush against the leafless, grey-green branches. The clusters of flowers are very simple. The four ruffled yellow petals, about half an inch long, may look like thin ribbon crinkled in the wet, but they are able to stand a sharp night's frost. The leaves are like those of an ordinary nut tree and appear in spring, with the added delight of fine autumn colouring. In October they turn the clearest yellow, especially in the variety *zuccariniana,* whose clearer citron-yellow flowers are an improvement on the more usual type. Winter flower and autumn tints make this a useful shrub. Too often we forget the autumn leaf-colour when we choose our plants.

Twenty years later came China's retort, *Hamamelis mollis,* collected by the great Charles Maries but left unrecognized for another twenty years in our English nurseries. It is surprising that we could have been so blind for so long. Finally, the sharp eyes of Mr Nicholson, Curator of Kew, spotted the beauty of its larger, unruffled, reflexed petals of clear yellow (the colour of forsythia) against the bare dark brown stems. Every twig was increased by grafting and soon it had won high prizes in gardening shows.

The pale lemon-yellow *Hamamelis mollis pallida* then appeared, probably the finest witch-hazel for your garden. It has the cowslip scent of its fellows but its petals are more delicate, a pale contrast to the characteristic red-brown neck of the flower. With patience you will grow a small tree 15 feet high. Even the impatient will get a generous show of flowers from a 2-foot-high young sapling. They stand out clearly against its leafless outline.

It was inevitable that the Chinese and Japanese plants should be forced into marriage by the hybridists. The best known results are the intermedia hybrids, especially the dirty red and copper-flowered Jelena and Ruby Glow. These are not to my taste, as the flowers do not show up well except when struck by winter sun with a dark green background behind them. This is not easy to contrive.

I prefer witch-hazels to be yellow and would like to put in a plea for the original American, *virginiana.* This flowers in October before the leaves fall and is thus thought inconspicuous and only regarded as an American stock on which to graft the Chinese. I like peering closely at a plant and do not mind a concealment of leaves over its green-yellow flowers. Its scent is good, and October is not an easy month for scent. Its autumn colour is the best of all. It is the source of witch-hazel for the bumps and bruises of childhood. It bears fruits and flowers together, hence *Hamamelis.* *Hama* is Greek for 'at the same time', *melon* for 'a fruit'. Even the ugliest names have a reason.

No witch-hazel needs pruning, but you can shape them into a tree if you wish by selecting one stem as 'trunk'. They are hardy and only blackened at the tips in the very foulest winters. Their scent is excellent indoors. They need a deep and rich soil in a dampish place if possible. In some eighteenth-century informal

Above: *Hamamelis japonica arborea.* Winter flowering. Best in light woodland shade and a leafy soil without lime. Propagation difficult

Below: *Hamamelis mollis pallida*. Slightly less robust, but likes same treatment. Not to be propagated by amateurs

gardens, the old *virginiana* is still grouped up on a mound or against an evergreen hedge where the flowers show up well. If you can give it a sunny site, you will enjoy it much more. And a whole grove would be a lovely planting. I see no reason why they should not flourish in the shelter of a city garden. They do not mind lime in moderation, but grow more freely without it.

If you have room for one big shrub and your soil is not too shallow and limey, try them out, continuing their history in your garden. There is no need to fear the witches that their name suggests. The Anglo-Saxon *wich* means 'supple' and hence the name for their bendy stems. Though their near namesake, the hazel, will indeed divine water, witch-hazels, I am afraid, are unlikely to divine black magic in your garden.

If you have always equated good gardens with the number or size of their flowers, winter is the season to make you doubt your logic. It is a time for twigs, bark and berries as much as for brightly-coloured petals. The range is wider than ordinary dogwood and cotoneaster. I would never have chosen many of the plants which now impress me in winter had I not visited the Cambridge Botanical Garden, reading that it had set aside an area for beds of winter shrubs and trees.

The snowberry is a case in point. On wet winter walks in a wood, I have always admired it, as it stands on the edge of a grass ride, showing a few of its white berries, like mothballs on its twiggy branches. But I would never trust it. In the garden it would sucker rapidly and barge its way out of confinement: its berries are too few for the space it would seize. It is described in dictionaries as suitable cover for pheasants. As a gardener, not a gamekeeper, that does not endear me to it. A bush like hawthorn, I thought, to be enjoyed in hedgerows only: I once grew a cutting of a small variegated relation but threw it away, perhaps overhastily, when it started sprouting an ordinary green.

But snowberries have since been brought out of the woods. They are now called *Symphoricarpos* and the breeders have been busy. At Cambridge, I was happily ticking off the old winter friends in flower: viburnums, winter honeysuckle, witch-hazel, but what were those 2-foot-high bushes smothered in round white buds? Inspection showed them to be not flowers but snowberries of a recent form called Hancocks. This is an improvement. Their berries are tinged with pink and borne in profusion. They will tolerate shade under trees but they give an even brighter show in a dry and sunny spot. A taller variety is called Mother of Pearl.

It is rare among winter shrubs to find one whose features stand out distinctively, despite the absence of leaves. This snowberry catches the eye at a distance, as if in full flower. It should not spread more than 4 feet wide, though I do not know a fully matured specimen. It does throw up suckers from the root but these are not uncontrollable and they have their uses as smotherers of weeds. A group of three would cheer up a dingy corner under tall and sparse trees. They grow anywhere.

Other excitements were no less easy to accommodate. Willows are one of my favourite families in the garden, especially those that do more than weep, and the patient gardener would find many rewards in the stems and furry buds of the small alpine kinds. At Cambridge there are two unusual willows of a different scale and attractions. Their branches seem to have been painted with silver paint and as both are still young, their appearance is slender and healthy.

The first, called *Salix daphnoides*, will eventually become a small tree some twenty feet tall. As with many free-growing plants on the borders between tree and shrub, I feel sure it would be possible to cut it back hard to its base in late spring and confine it to one year's young growth which would be all the thicker and shinier for the treatment. Its catkins are splendid and open to their full in February. All the while, its stems have this curiously frosted bloom on them which would show up so well against a dark hedge. At Cambridge, its neighbour is smaller and bushier and therefore more obliging. Its name is *Salix irrorata,* which means the dewy willow, a languid title.

Most surprisingly, it is a native of Arizona, the least dewy-eyed of landscapes. In a dry soil in the garden, it soon makes a tidy shrub, equally notable for this silvered effect of the stems. Its catkins have a touch of pink which is very appealing. If cut back hard, it would fit into a space about six feet wide, preferably in an isolated clump where the line of its stems would not have competition.

I would like to mass it on a grand scale across a sloping hillside

Right: *Cytisus battandieri,* Moroccan Broom. June–July flowering. Very vigorous bush to height of 15 ft and best on a sunny wall where it flowers freely; scented of pineapple. Will increase by summer cuttings, though they often wilt. Cut back after flowering as it is bushy on a tall wall. Likes lime

Right: Winter Garden in Cambridge Botanic Garden: orange-red twigs of *Salix alba 'Chermesina'*, grey bloom on twigs of *S. irrorata* and *daphnoides*. Prune hard in spring, preferably to base to encourage next winter's colour. *S. irrorata* need only be cut in alternate years. All these willows increase from spring cuttings out of doors

Left: *Rose Primula,* Incense Rose. Scented leaves: flowers in June–July. Will grow in semi-shade. Increase by cuttings or true suckers. No pruning, unless too big and leggy. 4–5 ft tall

with the stems of the Westonbirt dogwood, well described as sealing-wax red, and its yellow relations, *Cornus flaviramea,* each in their separate plantations. Apart from a pruning each spring, they would need no attention. Every winter, looking across to the hillside, I would see them as the spears of an advancing barbarian army, first, the silvered twigs of the willow, then, the red and yellow stems of the dogwood in squadrons behind them, bare and pointed in the winter's sun. This is not mere fancy as the long spears of Alexander the Great's army were indeed cut from cornelwood, cousin of the dogwood whose stem is reddened, as if dipped in an enemy's blood. There are no more appropriate shrubs for a field or large bank which needs gardening without trouble. Somehow such landscapes can take the ornament of winter twigs and stems more easily than the unnatural garb of many summer shrubs.

Where scent is concerned, plants are like people. Only if you know them intimately, handle them, look after them and even feed them will you discover their distinctions. The Moroccan broom, *Cytisus battandieri,* produces a short flower as yellow as a daffodil which smells of pineapple when it opens, ageing to boiled sweets as it fades. The small-flowered yellow *Clematis rehderiana* smells of cowslips. That unfamiliar winter evergreen called *Sarcococca* makes the January sunshine heavy with the smell of heather honey, if planted in groups of six or more. It flourishes in heavy shade.

Underneath a house window facing south, it is comforting to

plant evergreens especially in a small garden so as not to be confronted by bare decaying branches in midwinter. But winter green is better for a touch of grey and no grey-leaved plant is easier to tuck into a border than *Helichrysum angustifolium*. Damp, not frost, is a grey plant's enemy but I have grown this with great success on heavy clay; some sand round the roots when planting is always advisable. It grows a little over a foot tall, and at this time of year sends up 6-inch stems tipped by flat clusters of silver and yellow buds. Unlike some of its relations, it does not look better with the buds removed.

These open to a rather dirty yellow but the attraction lies not so much in its flowers as in its very strong smell of curry, most noticeable when the plant is brushed by a passer-by or rubbed in a disbeliever's hand. It combines most pleasingly with rosemary and gives an exotic uplift to less aromatic neighbours.

If curry sounds a little too adventurous, perhaps you would rather experiment with incense. I have not got a greenhouse at the moment and I cannot grow that wonderful annual *Humea elegans* in pots, bringing it indoors when its spire of red-brown flowers stands 3 feet tall and smells strong enough to lend an ecclesiastical flavour even to the most forbidding hall or passage. It should be sown in March, potted on as it grows rapidly, staked with a cane and enjoyed from autumn onwards. It can be slow and stubborn about germinating. Seed of this delicious plant can be bought from Thompson & Morgan of Ipswich. It will distinguish any drawing room.

Left: *Cornus mas*, Cornelian Cherry. Up to 25 ft × 25 ft: best when able to spread widely. Flowers in February–March. Very tough and easy in sun or shade. Will grow from hardwood cuttings but is not quickly or reliably increased. Any soil, including clay. No pruning unless too big. Above: *Clematis rehderiana*, grows vigorously and bears small flowers in August–September which smell of cowslips. Easily raised from seed

Right: *Humea elegans,*
Incense Plant. Half-hardy
annual, best in pots in
cool greenhouses.
Flowers in August–
September, scented like a
Catholic mass. Excellent
house plant. Sow seed in
March in high
temperature or with
bottom heat. Not too easy
to raise, but foolproof
thereafter

Outdoors, I very much enjoy a similar effect from what I believe should be called Rose Primula. Its stems are reddish and
thinly thorned. Its leaves, like those of many species roses, resemble a small acacia leaf drawn to scale. Again its flowers are
welcome without being very noticeable; pale yellow and an inch
wide, they decorate the ends of the shoots in late May. But it is
when rubbed or wetted that this humble rose comes into its own,
far outclassing its blowsier brothers. Soaked by the rain, Rose
Fragrant Cloud looks sorry and battered, shedding the petals
which have earned its name, but under the trees in the shade of a
shrubbery, 4-foot-high Rose Primula is spreading the smell of
incense far around it, its long-lasting leaves being brought to
their full scent by our usual June monsoon. There are more happy
hours for the nose in a Rose Primula than in a hybrid tea like
Josephine Bruce.

Oriental Curry, Papal Incense, all this sounds too exotic to be
true. But there is a patriotic note to end on. Our native *Iris foeti-
dissima* is well worth growing in a shady bed beneath trees where
its orange-yellow seeds can be enjoyed in winter. I am repeatedly
surprised how even the most knowledgeable of gardeners are un-
aware that its leaves when rubbed or broken smell quite unmistakably of roast beef. You should buy its variegated form, whose
foot long leaves are striped with cream, and then mass it beneath
an obstinate old tree.

Scents can be most elusive. By accident, I first squashed a leaf of *Geranium macrorhizum* and found it smelt of peppermint: nervously, I once twiddled a few leaves of choisya between my fingers and discovered that they left an acrid flavour which recalled the pungency of cheap gin.

Some discoveries have been pleasant; some Mediterranean cypresses, for example, smell like the pages of a long unopened antiquarian book. Others have been startling and repulsive. If you brush the leaves of the lovely Himalayan *Codonopsis,* their scent is thoroughly vulpine, the authentic whiff of a fox's earth in springtime.

This winter, however, I have added a new scent to my repertoire. I blush to admit my ignorance: for the first time, I have discovered how deliciously so many crocuses smell. I am well aware why I have taken so long to discover this elementary fact. I have always planted my crocuses outdoors and I have never tried crawling through them. I have also favoured what Reginald Farrer used to call the fatties, detesting them so much that the ink, he said, would clot on his typewriter whenever he came to mention them.

He meant those inflated Dutch hybrids which we all plant for a good show in the garden. When the sun shines, I do think the whites and yellows are pleasingly flamboyant, though the so-called King of the Blues is a blown-up purple-mauve which I never find congenial. It is worth planning their colours and keeping them apart. The whites show up well in shade, the yellows in sun-

Crocus medius. Flowers in mid-October, with lilac-blue petals

shine. They belong in drifts, not circles or mixed clumps.

Yet like so many hybrids, Dutch crocus have sacrificed scent for size. This winter, however, I decided to get to know more of the species crocus. It was *Crocus medius* which first surprised me, breathing a noticeable sweetness from its scarlet stigmata and lilac-blue petals as it opened wide in mid-October. Hopefully, I buried my nose in a nearby pot of *speciosus albus*. Though it glistened white, it did not reward me with a similar waft of honey.

Clearly, the sweet-smelling crocus would have to be hunted out with care. Since October, I had been hunting hard with varying success. December was certainly the climax. *Crocus longiflorus* was scenting my desk, while *laevigatus* was doing the same for the mantlepiece. Both are lilac-coloured and very delicate indeed. *Longiflorus* has most attractive markings of bronze. They both smell of heather-honey mixed with a hint of primroses, an extra-ordinarily fresh smell for midwinter.

The scent was carried on into the new year by *Crocus imperati,* another lilac-coloured flower whose outside petals are buff-brown marked with purple. It is gay and it is therefore no surprise to discover that it comes from Italy, being named in honour of an Italian botanist. But its scent is worthy of Paris, being more pungent and more subtle than any of its fellows. I had expected much of the bright yellow varieties which also were opening as the year turned but they were all a disappointment. Their colour was marvellous, especially in the *susianus* variety, whose long, pointed

Crocus longiflorus.
November flowering;
excellent in pans

flowers were backed with dark stripes, but none of them had the scent of their lilac relations.

I began to fear that *Crocus imperati* might prove to be the last sweet crocus of the crocus-year. Happily, the whites have come to the rescue in February, the lovely Snow Bunting to the fore. But again you have to discriminate. *Crocus biflorus weldeni* is also white and lovely but it does not seem to smell. Some of the *chrysanthus* varieties do have a smell, though often rather faint: Cream Beauty and Warley White seemed to me to be the most noticeable and I thought they smelt like hay when they began to fade. The common Dutch hybrids are out of the competition.

Yet the crocus has had the last laugh. I have been growing a variety called *graveolens* from seed: when its straw-coloured flowers opened out into a flat star, I hurried to smell it, full of hopes. It replied with a fearful stink, like a bush of elder or yellow broom. I now read that dried specimens can defile a room for years 'in much the same way as petrel eggs scent the drawer in which they are kept'. I have never collected the eggs of a petrel. But *Crocus graveolens* was a reminder that nature is not always kind to those who poke their noses into what is the business of bees, not men.

It is always comforting to be reminded that winter is bound to end and that the seasons will revolve for another year. Nothing reminds us of this better than the snowdrop of the February garden. But perhaps this is why this courageous plant has inspired more bad poetry and praise than any other. One glimpse of its snow-white flowers so early in the year and even the better poets lose their sense of proportion. 'Fair white maid of February' is prim enough even for Tennyson but 'harbinger of spring' is quite grotesque. However, there is at least a romantic legend which does better justice to the snowdrop's beauty.

When Adam and Eve left the Garden of Eden with thorns and thistles before them and a flaming sword on guard behind, the book of Genesis forgot to tell us that it was the depths of winter and the snow outside was falling thickly. The farther Adam walked, the more Eve dropped behind, resigned to a life of perpetual cold weather. Finally she fell down exhausted, whereupon an angel appeared before her; winter, he promised, would swiftly be followed by the spring and snowstorms were only a passing phase in the weather. Stretching out a hand for the snowflakes, he fashioned them into a snowdrop's petals as a pledge that spring would soon be coming on. Heartened by her new flower, Eve trudged on through the snow once more.

A very pretty story, but in my experience the snowdrop is rarely such an angelic gift as we gardeners have a right to expect. Though we all know it well, it is often a difficult bulb to grow with success. When happy, of course, it spreads into clumps that last for ever, outliving those by whom they were first planted. But either it likes your soil or it does not. There is little to be done to persuade it to flourish against its will. A dry soil is never suitable

Crocus chrysanthus Welden Fairy. A delicate species form for February; very easy

and manure proves fatal, I find. Shade and damp, leafy earth which will not get baked in summer, bone meal round the bulbs and competition, as in the wild, with the roots of other plants above, whether ground cover or grass: these are all to its taste. Safest of all are plants bought growing on in pots, not dry and dormant from the counter of a seedsman or supermarket store. But this is an expensive safety. The common *Galanthus nivalis* perhaps resents being planted dry from the packet less than most, but even then, what was planned as a clump in autumn may end up as a straggling line too thinly spaced in spring.

Though I have difficulty in persuading snowdrops to spread I am happy enough to treat them as rare bulbs. As I find it safer to buy my snowdrops as growing plants, I have felt justified in experimenting with the less obvious varieties. There are gardeners who devote a lifetime to their subtle differentiations. By now there is even a double form with yellow markings, the fussy Lady Elphinstone. These are too fanciful for me, but there are three unusual varieties which I would single out.

First is the Corfu snowdrop, *Galanthus corcyrensis,* which actually flowers in November. The leaves show through with the flowers, but otherwise you could persuade most gardening friends that this was the common February snowdrop awake six months too early. This is not difficult to grow. Next is the giant *Galanthus elwesii whittalii,* twice as tall (10 inches) with greyish-green leaves and a big flower with a green spot at the base and the tip of its

Galanthus nivalis and *Crocus aureus*. Ordinary Snowdrop and a free-seeding species yellow Crocus from Greece; as easy as a fat hybrid, but far prettier

inner petals. When wide open, its flowers remind me of an exotic fly. Last and best is *Galanthus ikariae* which only grows on one Greek island, the one on which Icarus is said to have collapsed when he flew too close to the sun. It is very small with bright green broad leaves and a dark green blotch on its outer petals. Its flowers come later than most in April, and are distinctive.

All these bulbs are particularly rewarding in a cold greenhouse. Plant them 3 inches deep and as much apart in September, and keep them damp and shaded till they flower. You can best enjoy the detail of the flowers this way, unspoilt by mud and rain. Many would not bring them inside the house without a qualm, but the monks of the Middle Ages believed their flowers would purify a room. The legend that snowdrops bring bad luck if brought indoors does not do justice to a flower which is said to have been made by angels.

The great days of private fruit are over and only a few private orchard-houses still survive from the past, at Luton Hoo or Warter Priory, for example, where fruit was forced to suit its owner's out-of-season whims. Fruit trees would be brought whole in pots to the dining-room table so that the guests could select their dessert as it grew. This elaborate ritual of the movable orchard has little to recommend it to gardeners today. But it contains a hint which I feel we all might follow up to our advantage.

It is the growing of fruit in pots which has attracted my atten-

Galanthus elwesii, at The Grange, Shelford, near Cambridge. A bigger Snowdrop, and a later one. By the broad green marks inside its 'petals' you shall know it

tion. Doubtless commercial fruit-growers practise it whole heartedly, but in the small private garden I have rarely seen it tried. Provided that you do not believe that your garden begins and ends with its flowers, a few potted fruit trees would make a striking impression outdoors.

Suppose you have a small front garden, paved or gravelled, or even a space on a balcony or roof; whether at office or at home, this would always be the better for a large potted plant and none is more enticing than a generous bush of fruit. First comes the blossom, then very elegant leaves, then fruit which is decorative as well as edible, for unless your hunger gets the better of you, a well-fruited apple tree is as attractive to the eye as any autumn flower. The polished green and red skins of its apples are much more subtle than a Michaelmas daisy. Determined to pot up a fruit tree and try for myself, I cast around for what gardening dictionaries call 'cultural hints'. Working on the theory that the Edwardians brought private fruit growing to its peak, I turned to an Edwardian book for advice.

Much the most helpful was written by a Mr Thomas and a Mr Bunyard in 1904. Their method of work was most amusing. Mr Thomas would describe the tarring and spraying, the back-breaking digging and the hazards of the ladder. Mr Bunyard would provide the epilogue, running through dozens of different varieties in a few masterly pages, describing their fruits and commenting crisply on their flavours with the expertise of a man who had personally savoured them all.

I could picture them in their orchard: Thomas in his braces, bustling from fig to early apple, tracking down the codlin moth and grumbling at the peach leafcurl; Bunyard in his deckchair munching his way through a Vicar of Winkfield pear and calling abruptly to Thomas for a Duchess of Oldenberg apple to take the taste away.

My picture, however, is a little unfair. Both were experts in their own right and Mr Bunyard was as industrious a grower as taster, presumably being a director of Laxton and Bunyard, that fine nursery which long continued his name. On potted fruit trees, their book is most informative: 'It is often said, and with much truth, that it takes years to convert a Britisher to anything novel or distinct, and fruit trees in pots are a case in point.' With the help of a Mr Hudson, they set out a powerful plan for its wider practice, explaining it in detail.

Trees are best potted-up in autumn, needing nothing more than a 10-inch-diameter pot. Modern plastic kinds would probably split, so be safe and choose a thick clay instead. Stable manure and a dressing of lime, preferably from old mortar rubble, must be added to a good loam soil. If a dry spell follows, the trees must be syringed to stop their wood shrivelling. By November watering and syringing can be dropped to a minimum. By the following spring, and increasingly as the fruit forms, the roots must never ever be allowed to dry out. When a potted tree is bearing fruit, it may need two waterings a day. Liquid or artificial manure should be applied in summer in moderation.

Fruits must be thinned progressively as they form and ripen: a tree in a 10-inch pot should be left with seven or eight ripe fruits and a tree which has borne fruit for two years should be given a rest in the third. Remember, however, that many fruits may be lost naturally between their first formation and their final stages.

Pruning is a matter of common sense; once the fruits are forming, the shoots can be trimmed back to the wood-bud next above the fruit. They can be similarly shortened throughout the summer. The vital point is that each tree should be repotted annually and that very seldom indeed do they need a larger size of pot. If a plant looks weak, put it in a smaller container. The old roots should be pruned hard with a knife in order to encourage young fibrous replacements. The ball of soil should be reduced so that you can fit your hand between it and the edge of the pot. Soak the roots, repot and top-dress with rich soil.

Fruit trees in pots will not be too quickly exhausted. They may last for twenty years, outliving contemporaries in open ground. They are much less prone to canker and insects. In a cold frame or greenhouse, peaches and nectarines (especially an old variety called Cardinal) can be satisfactorily fruited. Outdoors, plums and apples and even pears are very successful: the plums called Ontario, Cullin's Gage or Marjorie's Seedling, the apples called Charles Ross or Egremont Russet, George Cave or Cox's Orange Pippin are especially worth trying. Of the pears, Fondante D'Automne is recommended by the potting experts.

The great advantage of these potted trees is that they do not need enormous pots. It is this which could make them a very unusual addition to a conventional paved or courtyard garden. Good results take a little time, but if it means apples to hand from the drawing-room window or balcony, they are surely worth our patience. We may no longer be able to haul them into the dining room for guests, but it is still worth walking a few extra paces to taste and admire them for ourselves.

I have been asked recently how one ought to garden, and the form of the question surprised me. Garden as you please: that, of course, is very true. But some pleasures are wider than others and by comparing gardening with a sister art, I believe we can widen the sort of pleasure and results we aim to extract from it.

I have in mind a comparison with architecture. Gardening has often aspired to the ideals of painting, science or even sculpture. But now the word 'architectural' keeps cropping up, not only in the small talk of garden designers but even in nursery catalogues: what, if anything, does it mean, and do I think it useful? Comparisons between living plants and architecture can be made neatly, and, often, enrichingly. Try seeing the bare branches of an avenue of elms in winter as the pillars and tracery of a Gothic cathedral and you will, despite the high-flown simile, see them in a new and more congenial way. The comparison is a very old one, first used

Above: *Gunnera manicata,*
the biggest water plant.
Beware of frost: cover in
own dead leaves in
autumn. Will grow from
seed, surprisingly freely.
Must be in damp soil

Above right: *Onopordon
arabicum.* Biennial
thistle to 7 ft: June–July
flowers. Any soil, grown
for its silver shape. Very
easy from seed, and seeds
itself copiously

Right: *Eryngium alpinum,*
Donard's variety. Grows
to 2 ft in June–July. Likes
dry, sandy soil best.
Divides easily, or grows
from root cuttings taken
in spring. Seed is easy too,
but this good Irish variety
of the wild alpinum will
not always come true

by Italians of the fifteenth century to decry the rival Gothic architecture of Germany. Its pillars, they said, were rude and tree-like, reflecting on the barbaric way of life in a German forest.

But this is not quite what we mean by calling a plant or shrub architectural. We mean it has a firm and bold outline, stiff and pointed leaves, perhaps, and flowers of only secondary importance. It is a feature which is there, like a brick, all the year round, on which the gardener can build for the future. The spiky leaves of yuccas, so effective in London gardens, the outline of a dwarf willow, the leaves of the giant rhubarb or the titan of all water plants, my favourite *Gunnera manicata:* these are plants for the architect gardener and all the better for it. Most of them are evergreen and worth examining throughout the year.

I once read a chance remark by our greatest living landscape gardener, Russell Page, who has worked and lived for the most part in France. Though a stray remark, it seemed to me very appropriate. He described herbaceous and annual plants affectionately, but called them only so much gaily coloured hay. They are mostly weedy in shape and leaf, dead for half the year and alive with colour for three weeks or less. The annual cutting-down of the herbaceous border is indeed like the mower's scything of the grass and wild cow-parsley along our country lanes, that wonderful display which 'today is, but tomorrow is cut down and cast into the furnace'. It is luxuriant but it has no firm shape: it is here that these architectural plants come into their own.

And yet they have seldom been popular. In the first flush of herbaceous plantings early this century, discriminating gardeners compared their aims with those of the painter. They wanted, like Monet, friend of the gardening Miss Jekyll, to distribute their flowers' colours in drifts and original mixtures to form an impressionist effect. Miss Jekyll herself studied Turner and was influenced by her close friend Hercules Brabazon, whose watercolours were painted in careful tones to a special theory of colour. Architecture was seen, if at all, through a haze.

The most successful of these gardeners also recognized the importance of an architectural plant. The finest yuccas were to be seen in Edwardian borders, and I agree that we ought to garden nowadays by lessening this claim to be painters and trying to be architects instead. This means a farewell to the ideal of English cottage gardening which has often specialized in an excess of gaily coloured hay. It means a taste for body and bones, prickles, spikes and stems: it means introducing buttresses of yew (or box where space is limited) into herbaceous plantings and using them to hold the hay together out of season. Every long border should be divided into bays by evergreens and include some 40 per cent of plants chosen for firm and lasting leaves. We will be dropping our current taste for mini-irises, thumbelina sweet peas and knee-hi roses and welcoming back the giants, beanstalk and all. The 7-foot-tall silver thistle or onopordon may tend to dominate a border. Remove it, then, from a border and put it, like an

Above (in flower) and below (with seedheads): *Cynara scolymus,* Globe Artichoke. Over 6 ft tall in July; buds edible, especially in Vert de Laon variety. Best on sandy well drained soil which is

not ravaged by frost.
Worth protecting in cold
winters. Best increased by
divisions in April; seed is
easy, but random
seedlings' buds are seldom
edible

architectural feature, in long grass or a lawn and plan other plant-ings to fit in better with it at a distance.

The garden architect will find he approaches families of plants with a new and eager eye. The painter-gardener may like his del-phiniums (and so do I): the garden architect will bring back the despised thistles, the eryngiums, especially those with sword-shaped leaves and 5-foot flower-stems such as *serra,* the huge-leaved globe artichoke and the waving stems of fennel. Because architecture does not depend on colour, the architectural garden will be longer-lasting and, by the very nature of its plants, more firmly planned.

It will be full of evergreen rosemaries and evergrey helichrysum, especially the marvellous *fontainesii* form where the soil is dry enough to suit it. Its roses will be grown for their hips, like the wild *rugosa* varieties, and their thorns (like the tall *Rosa omien-sis pteracantha*) as much as their flowers. Plants will be set off individually as well as being massed in borders; they will be hap-pier, less in need of staking, less in need of cutting down and tidy-ing up. There will be evergreen fatsias, the sword-sharp leaves of phormiums, the huge leaves of rodgersias in damp places, a special place for grey-leaved sea kale and the red-leaved large rhubarb. It is, I think, the way one ought to garden. It answers the question from which I began, and yet it is still only what I think, not what law or logic requires. Gardeners are free to disagree, but architecture seems to me the most fruitful model for the man with a new garden and no point from which to start.

Thistles, Dr Johnson might have said, are a symbol for Scots-men and a food for donkeys. To gardeners, they mean sore fingers and tufts of down blowing into the strawberry bed, a prickly prob-lem for next year's croppers. But when I last walked across a stubble field, I looked at them closely and felt we had been unfair. Their prickly leaves spread outwards like a star which has fallen from heaven and been left lying face up on the ground. They have a bold shape and their prickles glisten in the rain. In a word, they have distinction.

This is not where we part company. Daisies certainly, elder-bushes possibly, but common thistles never, not even in a weed-ridden garden which we try to pass off as tolerant. They are too prolific to be given a chance. But they have many more respectable relations. Catalogues conceal the similarities for fear of scaring customers away, but there are some rare and original plants, not difficult to grow, which have the same prickly habit and downy flowers as the thistles themselves.

They would come in all shapes and sizes, some as small as *Carduncellus rhaponticoides,* which sends out a flat rosette of stiff leaves as a setting for its flowers, lavender-mauve like a tiny globe artichoke, others as tall as the onopordons, those invalu-able biennials with silver thistle leaves, 6 feet tall and like a huge pewter candlestick when given room to stand in isolation. They seed themselves from year to year.

In between I would scatter the annual Mary's Thistle, whose flowers are as nothing to its milk-white spotted leaves, the hooked and spiny *Morina longifolia* whose leaves are as nothing to its whorls of flowers, first white, then pink, then a blushing red when they have been fully fertilized. Like so many thistly plants, these hold up nobly when dead and can be used very strikingly in a bowl of dried stems and flowers. You can eat the buds of the thistly globe artichoke especially in the named Vert de Laon variety, and you can also enjoy its huge clumps of jagged grey-green leaves; you can pick the heads of the alpine thistle *Carlina acaulis,* which are disc-shaped and only a foot tall. You can match it with *Eryngium alpinum,* fluffiest and smartest of the smaller sea hollies.

So much for the outline of the idea. I feel that these angular shapes and prickles belong with the concrete yards and plate-glass windows of much modern building: their irregularity can redeem surroundings which are often left too flat. It is so fashionable for gardeners to think of planting profusely and mixing their flowers in the gay abandon of the cottage style. But the cult of the cottage is a curiosity which I cannot share. It can be as clever to plant too little as to plant too much. Style depends on the site and it should not be nostalgic in a place where cottage profusion looks untidy. Gardens should often be sharp and spikey as well as rose-embowered and honeysuckle-twined: there are corners and settings, I suggest, where thistles are not such an asinine taste after all.

Carlina acaulis caulescens. A dwarf stemless thistle for a well-drained soil; early summer flowering, pretty rosettes and spines. Easy from seed or divisions

March

One of the best ways to learn about gardens is to visit as many as possible. June and July are the climax of every garden-visiting year but the more you visit, the less you are inclined to leave your own garden and sacrifice one precious day in the weekend to somebody else's. One's own Bourbon roses are more special than their superiors at Sissinghurst: Hidcote's lacecap hydrangeas have nothing on the bushes you have chosen and planted yourself. Rather than miss the results of your own selections, you are reduced to garden-visiting in the lesser seasons.

It was in just such a mood that I made a visit to Hampton Court in March. I had come more to inspect the remains of Cardinal Wolsey's 280 guest-bedrooms, his arched kitchens and great court than to take in the details of the surrounding gardens. But even that worldly intriguing Cardinal had time for his garden amidst his cares of state: wheelbarrows, watering cans, 'pots for the 'erbs and twine to fix the arbours' all feature among the earliest accounts for his grand buildings. Visiting the palace gardens, very much later than the intimate style of Wolsey's own day, I was amazed out of season by a towering specimen tree.

In the winter sunlight, against the twirled and twisted Tudor chimneys, a gigantic *Magnolia grandiflora* had spread itself to the full. It must have been all of 20 feet tall and every inch as wide. Now March is hardly the accepted season for magnolias, largely because we concentrate our eyes and attention on flowers. It is an understandable prejudice, but with a little training and a little more attention it is easy to start noticing where before one had only been seeing and thus to pick out details of form, outline and reflection which the dedicated searcher for flowers would normally hurry past. To my way of thinking there is more beauty in a bush of ripe red currants than in the most floriferous cactus dahlia.

In winter, *Magnolia grandiflora* comes more in the class of a redcurrant. It has no flowers, only leaves. But the leaves are quite magnificent; they are as stiff and as long as a rhododendron's but without the ribbing or the deadening dankness of its well-known green. When *Magnolia grandiflora* is struck by the sun, it lives two different lives. On the leaf's upper surface, the light dances, reflected by shining green while the under surface gleams with ginger-brown, absorbing the light in its layer of natural fur. For if you turn over this magnolias's leaves, you will find them lined with pale suède, the colour of a country colonel's racecourse shoes. That alone makes it too good to miss in the garden.

Besides being evergreen, this king of all trees is also a magnolia. Among shrubs which flower, magnolias have no equals. *Grandiflora* is a late but long flowerer. In a warm summer, it begins to show signs of opening in July and does not finish until late October. The buds are like long white candles, hidden amongst the thick green leaves. Though you often have to search to find them, the more they unfold, the more unmistakable they become. The flowers grow huge, as much as a foot wide, with petals like very

smooth white wax held together by a central cluster of stamens.
They look too exotic to be true; even so, their final glory is untold.
Grandiflora's leaves may be fascinating, its flowers incomparable
among whites, but it is for their scent that they are enjoyed most of
all. On a late summer's evening, they overpower you with spices
and lemons and an ingredient of their own, like the smell of a
stone-pillared church, so cold that it makes you shiver even in
August. I cannot describe the strength of the resulting mixture; I
can only urge you to try it, if you have the room, for yourselves.
Often the flowers hold a nest of beetles who have come for the
pollen; they have enjoyed this, say scientists, since the world's
early days, for beetles and magnolias made friends before the bee
existed. Beetles always know where to go for the best.

In America, its home, this magnolia is free-flowering and free-
growing but in England it is so shy that it needs the shelter of a
good south wall. In the south, with other shrubs around it, it will
form into a rounded tree in an open position, but with young
plants costing over £3 each, I do not suggest you risk it in this way.

If you have a wall with a chimney behind it, that is the perfect
place: the chimney's warmth can bring a young plant through a
cold winter. But it will never hasten *grandiflora* into flower. For

Above right: *Magnolia
grandiflora*. Up to 40 ft,
less against most walls.
Flowers July–August. No
pruning. Will grow from
summer cuttings taken
from semi-mature stems
with a full ruff of leaves.
Needs 10 years to begin to
look its very best

Below right: *Daphne
odora aureo-marginata*.
Hardy in a bed against a
wall. Rather slow but very
easy to height of 3 ft × 3 ft.
Very scented flowers in
February–March.
Responds to an enriched
and gritty soil and
tolerates lime. Safest
when facing south.
Surprisingly easy to raise
from summer cuttings

that happy event, you must often wait ten years, allowing it to spread and thicken while you enjoy it as evergreen cover. You can sometimes encourage it by careful 'barking' in the spring, by stripping off a ring of bark near the base of the trunk and leaving a piece in the front untouched, so your scraping does not prove fatal; try to cut a circle, stopping before you make the ends meet. This restricts the flow of sap and encourages flowers, not leaves, above. If you do not fancy the risk, plant the Exmouth variety instead, which is shorter, quicker to flower and freer when it does so. Like all magnolias, it is best planted in April, enjoying an annual top-dressing of leaf-mould, protection in its first winter and plenty of water in dry weather.

'Call no flower happy until it's dead.' Even in the garden reputations rise and fall. Yesterday's favourite is tomorrow's abomination; bedding nowadays is out and the ferns of our forefathers are no longer visited upon us children. Tastes, of necessity, change and change is often cruel. To none has fashion been crueller than to *Bellis perennis,* the common English daisy.

The daisy's disgrace is complete. Her reward is a fortnightly dose of poison, her death a growth industry for chemicals and machines. Like all tragic heroines she has been brought to ruin by her own qualities. Imprudently, she began to grow too easily in grass. Obtrusively, she flowered from February to October. The Furies gathered, the shears snipped but the daisy refused to surrender. Where cutting and poisoning had failed, only hormones could humble and reform. Bellis must grow till she burst, victim of her own pride. Daisytox was born to kill her. There are, however, two sides to a tragic story. For centuries, the daisy was admired, prized for the very qualities we now revile. Lovers would appeal to her wisdom, children would turn her into chains and poets would praise the artlessness of her charms. She was even believed to exude a juice which would stunt the growth of dogs.

A dossier of daisy lovers still reads impressively, a list of sensibilities which are not to be despised. At its head stands Chaucer, Bellis's best friend, who called her the 'Emperice and flour of floures alle'. He would lie in the field to watch her open in the morning: he would return to see her close again at night, a peculiarity which earned her popular name: daisy is a corruption of day's eye. In the *Legend of Fair Women,* his Queen Alceste is turned into a daisy and retains as many virtues as the florets in a daisy-flower. The compliment is not to be despised, as the yellow centre of the daisy is a mass of these tight-packed florets, and what we would loosely call the white outer-petals are only a fraction of the total. Queen Alceste is a woman too good to be true.

Chaucer's example was not neglected. Ophelia in her madness, Burns in his coyness, Keats near his grave and Milton in his blindness, all showed favour for the day's eye's beauty. Thomas Hardy's wife adored it; Tennyson addressed it in four separate poems and Shelley considered it the pearled Arcturus of the earth.

Lilium auratum, Golden-rayed Lily of Japan. Up to 5 ft; no lime whatsoever in soil water or leaf mould. Likes woodland shade in deep soil. Should be planted 6 in deep and never left dry. Excellent scent. Increases slowly by bulbils

Wordsworth made two attempts, failing abysmally with one and rising sublimely with the other; 'A little Cyclops with one eye Staring to threaten and defy . . .' That was the secret of the daisy's success. From the tombs of the Egyptians to the floors of medieval monasteries, from the decoration of the Petit Trianon to Lady Beaufort's emblem in the Henry VII chapel in Westminster, *Bellis perennis* flowered its way into many responsive hearts.

But hearts began to harden. 'Oh, daisy, daisy cease thy varied song, a plant may chant too often and too long.' In 1831, Mr Budding's first lawnmower lumbered into attack. Wearied by the poet's praises, we were persuaded that henceforward, our daisies were better numbered. Flowers were better stamped out from the largest single area of an English garden and paradoxically, the most boring perennial plant in the gardener's dictionary, bent, creeping or browntop fescue, became the symbol of horticultural excellence. The English took it exclusively to heart, for all must be for the greenest in the greenest of all possible lands. If the daisy's downfall was hastened by her own persistence, part of the blame for her disgrace belongs to the society into which she was born.

Daisies, I suggest, are due for a revival. They need no mowing, manuring, spiking, worming, sanding or liming. They flower for seven months of the year, smelling sweetly and shining whitely, and they wear as well as those fine bowling green grasses which are named Emerald Velvet, as if velvet or emeralds were two materials upon which any sensible gardener would wish to walk.

Of course, a gardener is tied to the soil and to the length of his lawn, living with only an illusion of his freedom. But by coming to terms with the daisy, learning to love what advertisements ask him to abuse, he can cut through the worst of his labours, decking his hours in the grass with daisy-chains. For even the poisoners and grumblers admit, with a grudge, that *Bellis perennis* will have the last word. All go in the end to push up the daisies, however much they love and spray their lawn.

March is not a particularly easy time for a scented garden. The good smells of winter are going over. The long sprays of mahonia are dropping and rapidly dwindling to their tips. With me, it is too early for the Pheasant Eye narcissus, and common daffodils smell fresh but not powerfully. Late snowdrops and scillas do not really smell at all. Hellebores would not allow themselves such meretricious attractions; one is emphatically known as Stinking. Hyacinths, however, spread a heavy sweetness which carries far and is almost too much of a blessing; in death or nearby, they are repulsive. Neither primroses nor violets are at their best. I have never come close enough to a heather to know whether it smells or not. Maliciously, I suspect the worst.

However, spring has a smell of its own, especially on wet nights, and lured into the garden on a wet evening I find myself passing from scent to scent. It might be the papery smell of a cypress or the aggressive pungency of a bruised sprig of rosemary. But they are available all the year round. Another March smell attracts my attention more forcibly. It is not a very common plant, but I would always give it a home.

It belongs to that temperamental family, the daphne. This time it is not our native *mezereon* so much as a variegated relation which I warmly recommend to patient gardeners. It is *Daphne odora aureomarginata,* a 2-foot-high bush which eventually spreads to about a yard in width.

I first tried the ordinary *odora,* not caring for variegation and not realizing that it is often not very hardy. Two months later, it was killed by frost. Since then, I have grown to like gold-variegated plants, though my dislike of spotted laurel is as fervent as ever. Of them all, this daphne is my favourite.

Its gold is not so strident as that of a variegated elaeagnus nor so valuable as that of the admirable Privet. It runs round the edges of the pale green leaf and keeps the whole bush as interesting as any flower in summer. It is evergreen, of course. But March, undoubtedly, is this daphne's season of glory; the off-white flowers finally open among the tips of the branches, though their buds have been swelling magenta-pink for weeks before. They are small and rather tubular; their outsides retain the bud's bright magenta.

This daphne, as befits an *odora,* is the sweetest-smelling of its family. It smells supremely of spring but it is not a quick customer to please. It must be in a sheltered corner, preferably beneath a south wall, and must have a light soil, well laced with leaf mould. It can be grown prettily in a 6-inch pot. Drainage, as with most daphnes, is important, and when young, it should not be allowed to beg for water. Young plants move most easily. If you can afford to wait five years or more, do try it in a bed against the warm wall of the house, one of those narrow strips which we all have and which can be so difficult to fill. When you fling open the windows to begin spring cleaning, this daphne will charm you into inactivity.

What, wrote two gardeners from either end of England in the same week, would I do with a terrace? Thereby hangs a tale, for it is a most important part of the garden. Designers' jargon talks of it the way it merges the house with the air, but others see it more as an architectural feature which ties the skirt of the house into its surrounds and binds the whole building into the landscape. That is why houses on mounds, houses with carriage sweeps or houses where cars are allowed to drive on tarmac to the front door are not in harmony with their gardens. Yet many house owners run a drive straight up to their house's front, and encourage blobs of tin and metal, painted in yearly more tasteless colours, to interfere with what should be a terrace and part of the garden.

First, then, your terrace's solid materials. You may think I will stick out for York stone at £10 a square foot, being a thorough square, but in fact I do not really like it. It is notoriously slippery when wet and looks too like a pavement: I suggest you try mixing your materials in broad panels or in contrasting designs, the more adventurous the more you live in a town. You can even contrast colours, a blue or brown brick with a natural stone-coloured cement slab. Avoid mixing rounds and polygons with squares. There are calmer contrasts which never fail to please the eye, not least an arrangement of square panels of bricks in pairs, first set longways, then set widthways side by side and broken at regular intervals, every alternate square or so, by a slab of stone or stone-coloured concrete.

Be generous, too, with your terrace's depth. Grand French designers used to match their terrace exactly to the height of the house from the ground to the gutter. Few of us can afford to be so spacious nowadays and it is felt that the French carried things too far. But it is a useful ideal to bear in mind, for many modern terraces are mean little fringes.

Presumably, your terrace will be on the sunny side of your house so that you can sit on it. If so, you can plant at least half of your scheme with evergreens, knowing that they will be comparatively safe from cold wind and that they will give the terrace a feel of permanency whatever the season. There is a depressing defiance about sitting on a bare terrace when the first March sunshine opens the crocuses to their full width and brings the first bees to the daphne. Evergreens dispel this and they also help with the terrace's job of tying the house to its surrounds. No house could ever look stable when bordered with nothing but naked twigs.

Cistus is what you want, always growing fast and often delightfully aromatic; *obtusifolius* is low, small flowered (white, with a yellow spot) and perhaps the hardiest; a hybrid called *loretii* smells more of the Mediterranean scrub to my nose than any of the others; *cyprius* can reach 6 feet and among the hardier sorts it has the finest maroon blotch on its white flowers.

Cistus, then, at the base of your house or in among your paved panels, and with them mix a contrasting silver-grey leaf. There is still none better than the admirable *Senecio laxifolius* which needs pinching back every second spring to keep it compact and stop its nasty yellow flowers which look like a ragwort. If you are feeling adventurous, try the curry plant, or *Helichrysum angustifolium*, which has the finest silvery outline and does smell of curry when you rub it. A decided attraction, at least to my palate. Milder grey leaves can be enjoyed in a lovely low and spreading shrub called halimium, a fast and fairly hardy plant with which to soften a straight line of stone. Cold areas would be safer with a grey-leaved sun rose. The varieties of helianthemum named after Wisley will provide this, especially the pale yellow Wisley Primrose.

Allowing for winter sunshine, you can thicken up with the quick-growing, green Corsican hellebore, or *Helleborus corsicus*, and a mass of winter iris in suitably stony soil, perhaps with a clump of the white-striped leaf of *Iris pallida* in its variegated form. Rosemary, hyssop, white-flowered agapanthus, a mass of pinks for June (one called London Brocade, stocked by Ingwer-

40

Above: A well-organized terrace at Whichford House

Below: *Cistus* × *cyprius,* shrubby Rock Rose with aromatic grey-green leaves. Flowers June–July. Up to 4 ft and quite hardy. Likes hot, gritty soil with lime. Will increase slowly from summer cuttings

sen's nurseries of Gravetye, Sussex, has the old-fashioned laced look), not too many hebes, for their leaves are mostly dull in quantity, or too much lavender, for it looks too spiky out of season. Your terrace is acquiring a pleasantly evergreen balance.

Mild terraces could use some apple-green leaves of *Griselinia littoralis* or the wavy silver-edged leaf of *Pittosporum* Silver Queen, two distinguished shrubs which can be trimmed to order and should be risked in every garden, however cold, on the off-chance they will survive. Colder terraces can use a fig-leaved fatsia instead or the horizontal branches of the laurel called Otto Luykens which spreads to an eventual width of 7 feet.

And do not forget the tubular white flowers, sweet in scent, free in production, of April's finest evergreen, the osmarea. This too can be trimmed into formal banks or buttresses. And what about some clipped round blobs of box, not the ordinary green sort but the silver-edged variety called *elegantissima,* far too rare a shrub on the English country terrace? In a few gardens ordinary box has been used to fill in the space of a paved panel. A patch of box is planted below the terrace's overall level and only allowed to grow as high as the neighbouring paving slab before being sheared without let or mercy to give the effect of a green terrace square. I can imagine this looking very bold if contrasted with panels of spiky-leaved yuccas, those mainstays of the modern architect's garden.

Next, one of the more satisfying ideas for the pots and tubs which your area of terrace will need. It is a nearly hardy shrub called abutilon which comes in many forms, all of them looking very different and all of them excellent. I used to like a low-growing one called *megapotamicum* best. It has a wide and slightly pendent style of growth, well suited to the edge of a terrace wall and is one of the longest flowering shrubs I know, often continuing to produce its small flowers of red and yellow from June until December in a southerly corner. The shape of these small flowers is delightful. They hang from the stem in the manner of Solomon's Seal and remind me somewhat of a lady in a full-skirted evening dress, the yellow part being her skirt.

There is a variegated form whose leaves are splashed with gay yellow markings, perhaps a little sickly for those who have not yet adjusted their eye to the new fashion of variegation. Its flowers come in a more conventional bell shape of brick-orange; look for a form called *milleri*. These abutilons are quick growing, easily raised from cuttings or seed, often available in lists of otherwise tedious garden 'bargains' and hardy in southern or south-western aspects, except in the very coldest gardens. If you put them in a pot you can move them to a sheltered corner in late autumn. If you choose what are now my favourites, the varieties related to one called *vitifolium,* you might even build a greenhouse, so very precious you will consider them. They grow into standard shrubs, about 5 or 6 feet high, sparsely branched and thin stemmed. They grow fast, being slightly prone to frost, and are

Above: *Abutilon
megapotamicum.* Shrub
for pots or warm beds or
very warm walls. Hardier
than many think. If half-
frosted, can be cut back in
May. Very long flowering.
Will increase from
cuttings. Pretty as a
semi-standard shrub for
indoors

Top left: *Agapanthus*
Headbourne hybrid, hardy
form for borders. Flower
stems 2–3 ft high in August–
September. Likes sun and
enjoys lime. Very easily
raised from autumn seed

Bottom left: *Griselinia
littoralis variegata.* Shrub
for warm coastal gardens
and sheltered south-facing
beds inland. Excellent
evergreen leaf; well suited
in a large pot. Up to 4 ft.
No pruning

smothered in round saucer-shaped flowers of pale violet in early
June. Happily, they are beginning to become popular and nurserymen, especially Hillier's of Winchester, have hunted down improved forms. There is a white-flowered one, which I like less, a
very free-flowering one called Veronica Tennant, also pale violet,
and a decidedly tender one called Ashford Red which is a rare
shade of raspberry. In pots they give the height of a small standard
tree on your sunny front terrace, and these abutilons would be
most unusual and rewarding. They are members of the mallow
family, a guarantee of swift sappy growth and copious flower;
most certainly a plant to buy.

But, of course, they do not smell and if you have gone wild with
the cistus and other low evergreens you must have more scent
to waft you into a sensual paradise as you sit and plan your next
pay rise on a summer afternoon. Looking for cheapness, I suggest
you take instant action with a white lily called *longiflorum.* I
first grew this because I simply did not believe its catalogue description, any more than I believe in the myth of the 'trouble-free'
paeony. It will flower, said its suppliers, in its first year from seed
if sown in gentle heat in February or March. Bless me, it really
did. I had it pricked out by April, left it in order to get married in
June and returned to find it a mass of seed heads in mid-Septem-
ber. Rumour had it that it smelt delicious in my absence, and all
for 20p worth of seed from Thompson and Morgan of Ipswich. In
its second year it is even stronger, for some of those first-year
flowers are necessarily slender. It is also the most reliable lily
for growing in a pot in any soil. Gardeners in acid surroundings
or with a supply of soft tap water must also save up for a bulb or
two of the Golden Rayed Lily of Japan, or *auratum,* whose huge
spotted white flowers are heavily scented and too beautiful to
ignore. The bulbs should be placed at least 4 inches deep and
given a mulch of leaf mould, collected from trees which have not
been grown on limy soils. Otherwise the trace of lime left in the
mould will kill them.

You have scent and shape: all you need is body, which you can
find very quickly in the Tree of Heaven, or *Ailanthus altissima.*
The economical will grow this from its winged seeds, reminiscent
of a sycamore's. Others will buy it as a bush-shaped specimen and
have no scruples about cutting it ruthlessly back to its base every
spring in order to keep it as a squat shrub whose stems bear even
longer and more exotic leaves for being confined. As a tree, it will
reach 70 feet; as a shrub pruned to a height of 5 feet, it will throw
out yearly stems of long pinnate leaves, a glossy green which
might be mistaken for a superior sort of *Rhus,* such as autumn
sumach. Its flowers, which it does not produce as a trim shrub,
are no advantage, especially as they smell of burnt milk. Its shape,
again when pruned, is something which no keen terrace owner
should scoff at. Bushy, slightly tropical, fast-growing and a joy
for its fashionable foliage; who would have thought that a tree
would be happy on a small garden's terrace?

There are many pleasures in gardening and in early April none is stronger than the pleasure of expectation. A man next door is planting a Pocket Handkerchief tree. I have seed from a thing called eremostachys; two friends have been persuaded to try a clump of an evergreen called mahoberberis, whose holly-like leaves are blue-green and worth an experiment if you ever happen on them in a catalogue.

None of us knows how these new ventures will turn out, whether sooner or later, thick or sparse; if gardening was only a matter of repeating last year's marigolds or trying to make the asters fatter and shaggier than anybody else's, I would have given it up long ago. But every gardener likes to see a sign, and my favourite at this moment is the lilac. If you pick off a few of the green shoots from a lilac and press them open, you can judge how profusely it is going to flower in three months time. The sign is the number of shoots which contain small green flower buds, like a fish's roe, rather than a pair of furled leaves. If you choose an old bush which is normally shy to flower you can judge a good lilac year by the high proportion of embryo flowers in the shoots you test.

April is an excellent month for planting lilacs in well-drained conditions and if you have room for a pink Canadian hybrid with tubular sweet-smelling flowers or a mauve and white laced one called Sensation, the most unusual lilac in the book, you should send for a catalogue from Notcutt's, Woodbridge, Suffolk, kings of the lilac in England, and bully them or any other supplier if they write back with the excuse that the despatch season is over. Spring planting suits the lilac, as a heavy or badly drained soil can kill it off in a wet winter.

A more open sign of the times are the catkins on willows, pussy and otherwise: it is widely believed by surrounding villagers that a heavy crop of catkins means a dank summer, and as recent springs have been wonderful for willows I am inclined to believe they may have a point. At the moment I would almost trade the summer sunshine for the beauty of a willow. The common weepers are looking more lovely now than ever again in their season, having turned yellow along their stems with new life. One must remember that these admirable weeping trees do not absolutely insist on growing in damp places or on river banks, despite memories of the Psalms, Shakespeare's Ophelia and Japanese silk paintings. But they do eventually need width and height. Too often they are seen in a small front patch for which they will not be suited in fifteen years time. If you do plant a weeper by open water, remember that it will never weep symmetrically but will bend more towards the water because of the light which the water's surface reflects. Watch, too, for the scab which all too often attacks a willow's trunk and is best treated by spraying with a copper fungicide, available under any number of brand names at this time of year. It is this beastly scab, not melancholy, which causes the deaths among newly planted weepers.

Above: *Salix babylonica*, Weeping Willow, so named from the Psalm 'By the Waters of Babylon'. Will root from stems bedded into damp earth. Mature trees need space more than water

Below: *Syringa persica laciniata*. 4–5 ft × 4–6 ft eventually. Small lilac, scented flowers mainly in May. Trim lightly after flowering

Not that the weepers have obvious catkins to prophesy the weather. For these, and much else, I do urge on you the small shrub willows which are so seldom planted. Some, it is true, are slow growing, and I have not the patience for *Salix lanata, retusa, reticulata* and *stuartii* to go about their business to a maximum height of a foot. Their catkins, however, are beyond reproach and the woolly silver buds along their bare stems at this time of the year would be an ornament to any collection of alpine plants or stretch of paving planned for plants as much as pedestrians. They are architectural plants.

I fear that the pride and joy of a Mr Boyd, one called *boydii,* which he found growing wild on a Scottish hillside near Angus, is too small and too slow for me to do anything more than admire his sharp eyesight and leave it for owners of miniature gardens. But, and I blush for the name, a taller one called *wehrhahnii* is splendid. Three or four feet high and wide (eventually), it has dull plum-brown stems as a foil to its silvery catkins. If yours is covered with spring beauty as never before, up with your summer umbrella and prepare for the worst. Such willows say a wet summer, so there is nothing for it but to stock up your garden with them and hedge your bets by enjoying them instead.

April in the garden means daffodils and hyacinths, the first signs of wallflowers, the last signs of camellias, many a primrose, more polyanthus and a 20 per cent increase over last year's national quantity of forsythia, that infallible growth stock which was first launched in honour of William Forsyth, Regency England's expert in apple tree diseases.

But this spring I have been much struck by the forgotten herbaceous plants of early spring, when paeonies only show their clumps of thrusting red shoots and poppies have a very long way to grow. My favourites are not exotic. They would belong in the wild and woodland garden, were there any woods and wildernesses still being gardened in these days of cramped space. Copses filled with meconopsis, woodland ponds profuse with primulas: except for enthusiasts these are gardening dreams of the past.

Hence, I suspect, the disregard for early spring plants rather than bulbs. But lack of space should not deter us from applying a convenient idea on a smaller scale. These spring plants still have a place in a small modern garden in a wild, untended corner.

Their overriding merit is that they will flourish in shade. Take the doronicum, for instance, the Leopard's Bane of herbal legend; its cheerful daisy-flowers of yellow are common in continental Europe but few gardeners bother with them in Britain. But they are the most dazzling plant for the foot of a north wall.

The *caucasicum* variety is the pick of the bunch, partly because it is only one foot high, partly because its yellow is clear and its petals are free from any taint of orange. The joy of the plant is the colour of its accompanying leaves, a fresh lime-green which sets off the flowers in a bright and spring-like way. There is a double form, a tall form and a form called Miss Mason which is

Above: *Salix lanata,* Dwarf Woolly Willow. Very slow to about 2 ft. Long catkins, especially on females, in spring

Top right: *Polyanthus.* Best in damp soil. Remember the sparse autumn flowers which are pretty when picked. Sparrows peck the buds out of my plants. I am unlucky with the seed, but cannot bungle the easy task of division

Below right: A mixed border of forget-me-nots and tulips

said to be freer-flowering. My *caucasicum* are so generous that I doubt this. They do not like to become too dry in a hot summer.

Shade, even dry shade under small trees, will also suit that rampant, low-growing spurge called *Euphorbia cyparissias*. It is so free-growing that the faint-hearted might fear it as a nuisance, but personally I could never have too much of it and its excesses can easily be controlled by firm use of the spade. It is about a foot high with masses of stems, whorled and fuzzed with leaves like miniature Mare's Tails; they alone are of interest throughout the summer, and they colour a fiery red in autumn before dying down to a nest of small green buds like a stonecrop's. But in late April and May they are completely covered in clouds of green-yellow heads each containing twenty or more flowers like frogs' eyes. These are wide-eyed but not so heavy as the bigger and uglier spurge varieties. It is generous enough to grow under trees or as a filling in a narrow, difficult bed. Provided that nothing very delicate was too near it, I would give it a prominent place in my planting.

If yellow Leopard's Bane sounds too flamboyant, there are blues and whites of other spring families to tone it down. Blue-Eyed Mary, or *Omphalodes verna*, has long been a standby for the worst shady corners. It is some 3 inches high, quick to spread, fresh-leaved and innocent. It might well be mistaken for an early sky-blue forget-me-not. There is, however, a new variety which is even better: Anthea Bloom, a name indicative of its quality as it was first spotted in the Bressingham Nurseries of Diss, Norfolk, source of many fine plants. It flowers freely and accompanies its pale-blue show with leaves of grey-green. It would fit into any garden whatever its size.

Six-inch plants are easily lost in a jungle. Rather more robust is *Brunnera macrophylla,* like a forget-me-not in flower and colouring but unmistakably borage-like in its rounded coarse leaves. These, however, become an eyesore later in the year. I tear them off as soon as they become offensive and this does not seem to deter it. As it is some 2 foot high when in flower, it is well able to poke up through the spring grass of an orchard or in the tangle of a dark and weedy border: there, the leaves can be overlooked. Its near relation *Mertensia virginica*, the Virginian cowslip, is less rampageous but much more lovely. Commonly called blue-flowered, it combines indigo, purple and lilac, while its leaves are a subject in themselves. First they are black; then they are smooth and green, delicately traced with the lines of their lurid youth, like the face of a tired old *roué* whose make-up cannot conceal the past.

Yellow, then, and blues: to round off my spring selection. I need some imposing white. That is not difficult to find. In the gigantic family of crucifers, a botanical classification which covers a mass of garden horrors, there are three shade-loving white ladies of April, any of which deserves a place in a corner of spring plants. Their names are *Dentaria*, *Hesperis* and *Cardamine*, rather like a

Doronicum caucasicum, Leopard's Bane. April–May flowering wild herbaceous plant. Any soil, sun or light dry shade. Very easily divided in autumn

trio of pale sisters from a Gothic fairy-tale: in English they are more vulgarly known as Toothwort, Sweet Rocket and Lady's Smock respectively. They are all about a foot and a half tall: I like *Cardamine trifolia* best, as white as any lady's petticoat and perfectly content in a damp, forlorn bed. Omit its double form.

The Sweet Rocket is lavender-white and is not easy to establish in town gardens: that is a shame, as it has the delightful habit of smelling most sweetly towards evening. *Dentaria pinnata*, like all these spring flowers, has large, fresh-green leaves; unlike coarser companions, these dwindle away as summer gets into its stride, leaving a gap to be filled by lilies or hardy annuals. I wish it were planted as often as the yellow alyssum to which we turn out of habit as much as taste.

Of all the seasons in the garden, spring is most liable to fall a victim to habit: these spring-flowering plants are a rewarding way to break out of the ways in which we have always gardened before.

Difficult corners are a part of every gardener's life. Even in the smallest garden, there is a bed where gutters drip, cats settle, trees obscure or earth goes a mere 3 inches deep. Sometimes, there is little else to compensate, especially in cities. But though it is almost impossible to make these corners flamboyant, they can be turned into features of interest. It is here that knowledgeable gardeners start with the advantage. Out in the sunlight, ignorance is often a blessing, leading to most felicitous results. But deep in a shady corner, the range is more limited and chance choices less likely to succeed. Each adverse circumstance needs different treatment. The admirable white valerian is prolific in dry shade under trees, but it is not a plant for those who are menaced by congregations of cats. Its feline appeal will only make the problem worse. Musks and primulas thrive in the damp; in the dry, they dwindle and disappear. A Christmas rose needs deep soil, a periwinkle does not. Difficult corners cannot be solved on paper. But there are ideas which are wide enough to meet most situations.

Several are at their best now in early spring. It is these which I would like to reconsider, none more than *Pulmonaria*, Spotted Dog. On the evidence of its spring display, I would plant it in any problem corner and know that every April it would reward me. Its flowers are true bright blue and it forms a spreading mat of leaves from March onwards, holding its flowers 6 or 9 inches high. It is so easy, generous and infallible that it would win every horticultural prize but for one dreadful failing: after flowering, its leaves grow larger and coarser until you long to tear them off in desperation. But gardeners in difficult corners cannot be too choosey. The *angustifolia* variety is better than its even coarser brothers and sisters, and for three months of the year, it is most acceptable. I think it is too valuable to be ignored.

Spotted Dog, then, at ground level, intermixed with white violets, lily of the valley (best in the Everest variety), some aconites perhaps, a hosta or two and a free-flowering bergenia, perhaps the modern hybrid Silver Light. I do not care for bergenias

Chaenomeles speciosa, Flowering Quince. April–May. Should be cut back hard after flowering or pruned hard on wall. Any soil, any site; likes lime and tolerates shade. Varieties range in colour from red to white, in height from 3 ft to 8 ft

which do not flower. This mixture should succeed in most of the gardener's problem corners.

But what about the next level, the bulky 4- or 5-foot-high masses which give the impression of luxuriance? These are by no means easy to find. I would like to try the golden elder, as a brightly coloured leaf is always a bold retort to the challenge of dark gardens. Sometimes it is said to be too out of the way to be grown in unpromising beds or backyards but I have not found this to be so. I know three bushes in three different counties and each is content with a dark, dripping position.

It is a shame that it is not more widely planted, but unsuspecting gardeners are deterred by its name: *Sambucus racemosa plumosa aurea*, in its most worthwhile form. This will grow to 6 feet in poor soil, though it is a slow mover; when fully grown it continually catches the eye. Its leaves are golden-yellow and finely cut, so graceful that you forget its rampageous hedgerow cousins.

There is also a *Sambucus nigra aurea* which is almost as golden but not nearly so delicate. It is an infallibly strong grower but in its haste, it is coarse. For a very difficult corner indeed, it would certainly be worthwhile, but otherwise I suggest you patronize the tongue-twisting cut variety and wait with patience. The coarser kind only colours brightly in sunny beds.

Spotted Dog and so forth on the ground, golden elder above them: all my suggestion needs to complete it is a tough and reliable climber. In light shade, away from the drip of trees, I would certainly go for a flowering quince, or *Chaenomeles*. These favourite wall plants flower thickly on leafless branches in April, adorning their nakedness with ruffs of pink, red or white flowers like hawthorn. It is important to prune them in May after flowering.

Behind my golden elder, I would try the pink-and-white form called Apple Blossom: its name is self-descriptive. In extremely heavy shade this would not be likely to flourish. I would therefore pick up the elder's colouring by planting a golden variegated ivy behind. The form named *Hedera colchica dentata variegata* is as striking as any. The result would be gay and golden, exactly what a problem corner needs. As in life, so in gardening; defiance is the answer to despair.

'In our perambulations we had come to a place where the Snake's Head fritillaries hung their chequered bells. Every Oxford man worth his battels knew them in the month of May round Iffley village or the meadows beneath Cowley, a symbol of the best of the year, the best of the years maybe. In my time the most unlikely sorts of men would pick them from bunches glowing among the grass like green fire. We would come laughingly down the tow-path with our spoils; they may do so still when Finals are afar, the boat runs well and ladies are coming up for the Eights.'

I am happy to report that they do not, for students are not such vandals that they treat our wild flowers as spoils for the picking. That was all very well for the 1890s to which these quoted reminiscences belong, days when faces were fresh and undergrads were all clean-limbed, when clocks still stood at ten to three and when there was no British motor industry to rape the suburbs of Oxford; there never was a greater swell than the captain of a pre-war boat race crew.

But despite his sentimentality this old man had chosen his subject well. No flower is so mysteriously lovely as our native fritillary. The legends say it grew from the blood of those massacred in France on St Bartholomew's Day in 1572. Nobody would believe that, but in fact a young English apothecary from the Midlands did pass over the field of the massacre soon afterwards and was much impressed by the wild 'snakeshead lilies' which he saw there.

He had some shipped by a French merchantman to England and later grew them successfully in the garden. Had he known better, he probably would have found them growing wild already in this country; certainly they were known to the Tudor herbalist Gerard, 25 years later, who was at a loss to describe their unique quality.

Aptly he remarked that they were finer and more curious than the best of paintings. Fritillaries do indeed have an artistic air about them, a colour and texture that would be well at home in the foreground of the most exotic Carpaccio painting. This colour is notoriously hard to describe and varies from bulb to bulb. Generally, they are 8 inches high with one, or even two, hanging bells of six petals, each marked inside and out with a check pattern of purple and white alternating squares. Inside, the colour runs darker round two central yellow stamens; the stems and very thin leaves are a flattering shade of grey-green. The petals are of a solid texture that feels like close-cut apple peel.

But any description is bound to be clumsy for the fritillary has such a mixture of qualities. For once, the Latin name is more instructive: *Fritillaria* (from the Latin for a dicebox), *meleagris* (from the Latin for a guinea-fowl), a subtle compound, for the flowers do hang like a down-turned dicebox and have the colouring of a guinea-fowl's feathers. The Germans, less appropriately, call it Plover's Eggs, which are a different shade. Country people once feared the fritillary as a plant of doom and gave it rude or ugly names like Weeping Widow or Toad's Head. But standards change, and keen gardeners value them and their Far Eastern cousins as the most distinctive May-flowering bulbs. In the garden they must have a wet soil to give their best. They are happy on lime: in a waterside meadow beside a stream or in a wild wet garden they will run and spread freely in hundreds and thousands. They can compete with the toughest turf. If you have a damp place, plant them 2 inches deep in autumn. They could hardly be easier to grow. Slight shade suits them better than sun.

Sadly, I live on a hot, dry soil which fritillaries do not enjoy for long and in order to grow my favourite bulb I have had to grow it in pots instead. Here it needs excellent drainage and some leafy earth in a deep pot, for the roots become very long very quickly. Again, plant them 2 inches deep in autumn and leave them in a

Fritillaria meleagris, Snakeshead Fritillary. 9 in high; bulb. Flowers April–May. Persistent only in damp soil. Likes water-meadows where it naturalizes itself and spreads freely. Increase is otherwise a forlorn business. Plant in Autumn. 2 in deep above top of bulb. The white form is above; right is the white and purple mixed

cool, dark place for at least eight weeks. Then, gentle heat will bring them into flower in late March. Though the bulbs in pots last well for only a year, it is worth bothering with the more expensive varieties. Aphrodite is a very large white; Charon is dark purple; Artemis a pretty pink-grey and Poseidon a rather unreliable white marked with maroon. All are worth trying, except the *contorta* varieties whose flowers are shaped like tubes and seem to me to have lost the charm of old *meleagris*.

Essentially, however, these are not bulbs to be confined in captivity, as anyone who has seen them in nature will know. In a pot the flower's markings can be admired at leisure, but in the eight or nine English meadows where they grow wild the mass effect of thousands is amazing. One of the principles of good gardening is to plant in generous groups, but nature can be more generous than even the most extravagant gardener.

In a meadow in the middle of modern Oxford they are still growing in their thousands, possibly the most dramatic sight in the world of English wildflowers. All around, lorries thunder down their smart new ring roads and dons try to approve concrete blocks in which to house their students. After another seventy years' technology those fritillaries may not be there to remind the 'most unlikely sorts of men' of the very best of the year.

When I say that fritillaries are my favourite flower, I am often asked which fritillary I mean; the answer is our native Snake's Head, chequered and sombre, bowing its flowers modestly among the simple line of its grey-green leaves. But the question is a tribute to the whole family, for there are many other fritillaries, any of which might well be a gardener's favourite.

I have recently experimented with certain rare relations such as *citrina* and *pinardii*, neither of which I recommend. One variety, however, cannot be so negligently treated, *Fritillaria imperialis*, better known as the stately Crown Imperial. I would like to present a case for its wider use in gardens. Dictionaries and handbooks still refer to it as a common plant which thrives in cottage gardens, but as I suspect that cottage gardening is fast becoming a myth (though books are now being written on its range and history) I feel justified in urging you to reconsider it.

Among spring bulbs, it has the advantage of being tall, reaching 4 feet by mid-April and thus providing a statuesque background to primroses, anemones, dog's tooth violets and other smaller flowers which grace the ground at the same time. Not only is it tall: it is extremely striking, with an exotic air which befits a native of Persia. Its stem is thick with green fleshy leaves, set so like a lily's that early botanists included it in the lily family, a classification which still holds good.

At the head of the stem, the leaves are gathered in a thick top-knot, reminiscent of the top of a pineapple but less rigidly arranged. Beneath this green top-knot, the flowers hang in bunches, shaped like the diceboxes from which the fritillary took its Latin name. Broadly, it comes in two colours, either yellow or brick-red, though many intermediate shades from pale lemon to outright orange have been selected and named. I prefer the brick-red sort, especially as daffodils provide enough yellow already in spring.

With all hanging flowers, especially fritillaries, the first temptation is to reverse nature and hold the petals up to peer inside. With the Crown Imperials this is a mixed blessing, for as soon as you brush against it, it gives off an extremely strong scent of fox. But if you do not flinch from the smell you are rewarded for your troubles. Inside each hanging bell, in the roof of the flowers, are set six white spots in a dark surround. Botanically, these are the nectaries of the Crown Imperial. Historically, they have been fair inspiration for some baseless but charming speculation. Like many flowers, the stately fritillary has gained more from our imagination than from sober science.

Most famously, these spots have been seen as a punishment for atheism. It is said that alone of the flowers at the Crucifixion, the Crown Imperial refused to bow its head in sorrow, feeling that Jesus had got what he deserved. When proved wrong by the Gospel tales of the Resurrection, it lapsed into an eternal blush, changing its colour from white to orange, hanging its flowers earthwards, and retaining six white tears of repentance inside them as a confession of its error. That, however, is a slander made up in

Christian countries; the Crown Imperial reached Europe through Constantinople, being distributed in the mid-sixteenth century by the Duke of Florence's personal doctor. It originally came from Persia where it was eaten as food and dignified with a more favourable legend.

An Empress called Atossa was wrongly suspected by her husband of infidelity – faith was clearly not the Crown Imperial's strong point – and was changed into an Imperial Fritillary instead. As a symbol of her unjust treatment, she shed six tears which are thus perpetuated at the base of her flower. Gerard the herbalist even believed the spots were made of imperishable water. He cannot have looked very closely.

The Crown Imperial is more than a memento of man's unscientific way of thought. Except in sandy soils where it can prove difficult it is an obliging early border plant, happy at the foot of a hedge or in a shrub bed where it will not be spiked with a probing fork during its dormancy later in the summmer. Like all spring bulbs, it should be planted in the autumn. It is happy in heavy soil, provided that it does not become too waterlogged in winter, a danger which can be avoided by planting the large bulbs at an angle to one side.

If I asked you to a party to come and see my cherries you would probably refuse, suspecting a double entendre; it was not always so. Parties in honour of cherry blossom were the height of civility in Imperial Japan, where a fine show of flower was the test of a gentleman.

'From five to six miles I walk every day in search of you, cherry blossoms,' wrote the most sensitive of Japan's travelling poets three hundred years ago; nowadays, for five miles around my garden, such a walk would only reveal a mass of raspberry-pink blossom, mostly of the kind called Kanzan which was never prized in Japan. We are much too timid in our choice of cherries; when I walk round inspecting some of the more adventurous plantings their variety amazes me. Cherries will weep, stand upright like sentries, spread like umbrellas, flower from November till May and bear blossom of any shade from pink lipstick to greenish-yellow, like a primrose.

But were there ever bullfinches in Japan? I would very much like to know, because an Englishman's sense of melancholy on seeing a cherry in springtime is caused more by the raids of sparrow and bullfinch than by the brief life of its flowers which so moved the Japanese. It is almost, not quite, worth growing a cherry tree in order to see a bullfinch set about stripping off the buds, an extraordinary effort of acrobatics, mischief and skilled application of a curved beak.

To be fair, the bullfinch does destroy insects, which we call pests. I would never bother with any of the bird-repellents on the market because they have to be applied regularly from autumn until early summer and if they fail, as they do, it is always because on a chilly afternoon in March you happened to miss the

Above and below left:
Prunus serrula Tai Haku.
Flowers April–May. Up
to 20 ft × 15 ft. No pruning
needed

Above: *Prunus* Mikurama
Gaeshi, the Royal
Carriage Returns, now in
the Savill Gardens.
Astonishing, from this
photo, what would cause a
Japanese Emperor to
reverse, but it is an
imposing cherry-tree

topmost cherry-branch, thereby spoiling the tree's defence. Instead I would be inclined to try mothballs. Hang a few on prominent branches during February, and the smell of naphthalene is probably the reason why two growers who use mothballs tell me that for the last three years they have not been bothered by the bullfinch. 'On seeing mothballs hanging in a white-flowered cherry tree': I leave you to compose a suitable Japanese four-line poem, perhaps with the help of the Penguin translation of the admirable poet Basho, which explains the simple rhythms needed.

The choice of a cherry tree is never easy. I know I hate Kanzan, that blowsy, street variety of raspberry-pink which has about as much elegance as a geisha girl in full cosmetics and face powder. My favourite, of the obvious kinds, is Tai Haku, the largest-flowered cherry grown in England. Being white, it is also the most sensational. It is said, from what statistics I know not, to be less prone to the plundering of birds. It also has a nice story.

Tai Haku, or the great white cherry, as its Japanese name means, was thought to be lost to cultivation sixty years ago. On a visit to Japan, the Kentish king of the modern cherry tree, Captain Collingwood Ingram, was being shown antique paintings by a Japanese collector, and was much struck by a 200-year-old picture of a white cherry which his Japanese friend admitted had never been seen in Japanese gardens.

Artistic fancy was being invoked, when Collingwood Ingram remembered cuttings he had taken from a particularly large white cherry in a Sussex garden and which seemed a mystery for the size of their April flowers. Japanese drawing and Sussex survivor were compared and at once identified. From one English cherry tree, whose arrival from the East remained obscure, the world's growing stock of Tai Haku has been raised. If you can spare a 20-feet-wide, 20-feet-high space for a tree with a ten-day season, then plant it, with due tribute to the Captain's scholarship. Better still, plant an avenue.

The pinks, too, have their stories and their most unusual tree is called Mikurama Gaeshi. There is a reason for this. The Emperor of Japan was going to take tea with a lady whose fine handwriting had impressed him. Out drove the Imperial coachmen, postillions and Masters of the Fan down one of those bumpy roads which limited a day's travel to a mere five miles and made Japanese court life as enclosed a world as a modern city at six o'clock in the evening.

On a bank on the Emperor's right grew an upright sort of cherry, ungainly had it not been for the way it bore its apple-pink flowers. Each bud lay close to the branch and showed no stem; the Emperor, who had never seen a forsythia or a delphinium bearing flower branches in the same sort of way, noticed it and ordered the carriage to reverse.

Tea with the ladies was as nothing to an unusual pink show of blossom; the coachmen coughed discreetly, the horses were reined back over the ruts, and His Imperial Dignity, Child of the Chrysanthemum, Son of the Sun, inquired the cherry's name. It hasn't got one, they told him, and when he ordered them to find one, they suggested Mikurama Gaeshi, the Royal Carriage Returns. On drove the Emperor, resolved on a cutting; tea was late, and although it is not the most beautiful shape or colour among cherries, the tree he saw, growing 15 feet wide and high, is not one I would ever omit from a garden of spring blossoms.

Princess Mary, the Princess of Wales, the Duchess of Sutherland, Comte de Brazza, the Duchess de Parme, Govenor-General Herrick, Mrs David Lloyd-George, Admiral Avellan, Mrs Norah Church and Mrs J. J. Astor looking as pretty as ever . . . No, not a list of those, among others, whom I met at a very enjoyable tea party in the president's tent at Chelsea Flower Show. Instead, just an extract from the Who's Who of the English garden violet. No other country in the world could have given such exclusive names to the slight variations in such a tiny flower. Whatever the botanists do to their Latin, in the English garden there are always society names to be dropped.

At first sight, few flowers seem less blue-blooded than the violet. In woods and hedgerows all over England, six varieties grow wild where they please; in the days of flower-girls, violets sold for a penny, the least aristocratic of bouquets. Nevertheless, this native commoner can trace its family tree far back in time; 2300 years ago, Theophrastus, pupil of Aristotle and father of botany, remarked that the most skilled gardeners of his day could persuade the violet to flower in every month of the year. He was referring to our native sweet violet, *Viola odorata,* and though we do not have the climate of ancient Greece, in the West Country, at least, this charming wild flower is often out as early as November, continuing until April and early May, the months with which it is more usually associated. Those of you with room to spare in cold frames and greenhouses can still imitate the ancient Greeks and plan your violets to flower whenever you wish: slight heat forces them along very quickly indeed.

However, these wild commoners have no claims to a place at the violets' high table. The plants on my social roll-call are a very different matter indeed. The Duchess of Sutherland is an upper-class beauty: long and spindly in habit, rather fussy about where she goes, insisting on rich food but rewarding her friends with magnificent semi-double flowers. The large outside petals are a pure uncompromising blue but the middle ones are a subtle shade of pink. Like many violets, she has extremely good leaves of dark green. The Germans have renamed her Pride of Frankfurt.

She still has the edge over Princess Mary, another semi-double, whose outside and central petals are both rich blue. Mrs David Lloyd-George is easier to please and prepared to put up with poorer soil; her semi-double flowers are an attractive mixture of blue and gold.

Fine though the semi-doubles are, the full doubles are even

better. The Duchess de Parme has light green leaves and flowers of that shade of lavender which always reminds me of old ladies; the Comte de Brazza (who sounds like her hot-blooded lover) grows exuberantly with double flowers of racy white. But neither of these foreign grandees beats Mrs J. J. Astor whose dusky pink colouring is indeed unique: she is not too easy to please and is happier in a shady place.

The others are not so well-bred but they flower earlier in the year. Governor-General Herrick is regularly out in February and is extremely easy to grow. Like all these named violets, his flowers are bigger and more clearly coloured than the wild hedgerow varities. Like the Princess of Wales, he is royal purple, but he also has a very good smell which she does not. If you want to try violets in pans in a cold greenhouse, he is the one I would recommend as he flowers so early that he needs protection from foul winter weather. In a cool room indoors he makes an original alternative to the poinsettias and cyclamen of early January.

Of all the early varieties, however, Admiral Avellan is much the best. It grew excellently in the late E. A. Bowles's great garden near Enfield, where its purple-red flowers on long stems stood clear of their leaves and spread their true violet scent far and wide on clear February days. I have never seen it elsewhere but it is always known as an extremely easy variety. Mrs Norah Church (who does she think she is, anyway?) is more ordinary with dark violet-blue flowers.

Clematis alpina. Flowers April–May. Climber for west or cooler walls. Prune when necessary

All violets are better for some leaf-mould and fertilizer rubbed into their mats of leaves after flowering. Between paving stones or in cool places they are especially good because the earth round their roots is kept damp. None of them mind shade: all the aristocrats are evergreen, can be divided with care and thus make a first-class edging plant in any garden. The advantage of named varieties is that the stems are longer and the flowers are not hidden in masses of leaves.

'When violets grow on brambles...' was a Greek poetic proverb for an impossibility and with the blue-blooded beauties I have suggested, one can hardly imagine it being fulfilled. But they are ideal for the small garden of today. There is some amusement in growing two duchesses and a scattering of princesses in a small flower bed. Mix with a better class of violet while you can; Arthur Bottomley, Tony Benn and Mrs Barbara Castle: these will be the new Lilliput asters to fill the gardens of tomorrow.

No garden is complete without its sentimental corner. Nowadays we frown upon sentiment, feeling is suspect and those little touches of expression which delighted our great-grandfathers are thought to be foolish or merely patronizing. But the two prettiest garden plantings I have seen for some while were both of them sentimental. One was on the grave of a neighbour's dog, where a large urn had been planted with two double-flowered alpine clematis, the pink and slate-mauve forms of *Clematis macropetala,* and allowed to intertwine before falling forward over the stone slab.

In this unlikely site, they made a delightful pair of harmonious colours and had a suitably melancholic air. Too seldom we plant two differently coloured varieties of the same plant and allow them to mix naturally. I do recommend this combination of clematis to the owners of any urn, low wall or shrub which can take a climber over it. Their mood was not interrupted when around the corner of a nearby hedge there spread a huge planting of forget-me-knots. For there is no flower with a more sentimental history than a forget-me-not: once told it, no gardener who cares for a story will ever pass a forget-me-not by.

It all began at the end of the fourteenth century, when the future King Henry IV was still living out his Part 1 and most Englishmen were eating one-tenth of the food they now insist on. At court men had time to be romantic, the more so since they often travelled and fought in France. To please his supporters, the young King Henry, then Earl of Derby, began to wear the flower called *Souvenez Vous de Moi,* the French for our forget-me-not.

Wearers of the flower, he told his barons, would never be forgotten by their lovers, and such was male vanity that the thought of a lasting memory among so many women attracted the nobility and made Henry's suggestion into a fashion. He even ordered his tailor to embroider him a robe with a collar of blue *S*s, standing for Sovereign and Souvenir, remembrance, therefore, of the blue forget-me-not.

Silver thread was used to suggest the plant's leaves, and so

Fritillaria imperialis, Crown Imperial; bulb. Flowers April–May. 3–4 ft. Plant in autumn, tilting the bulbs on soggy soils. Increase only by offsets. Likes sunshine

Overleaf above: *Viola odorata.* Sweet Violet. Flowers in April, 6 in high. Likes shade, even dry shade. Easily divided or increased by its own runners. Not easy or quick from seed, at least with me

Overleaf below: *Clematis* Nelly Moser. Climber for west or lightly shaded walls. Flowers from May onwards. Likes shade at the roots, sun or clear light at head. Feed with liquid manure when buds form. Prune by thinning when necessary; cuttings will root with care

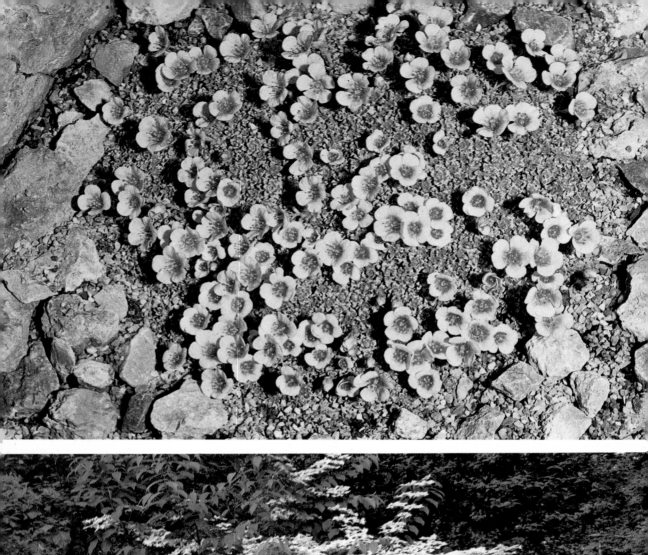

distinctive was the result that the emblem *S* became a recognized proof of allegiance to the House of Lancaster. The Lord Mayor of London still wears a collar of *S*s in remembrance of a Lancastrian benefactor. However, was Henry's French forget-me-not the same as the plant we call *Myosotis,* meaning mouse-ear, because the leaves once reminded some insensitive botanist of such an unattractive piece of nature? There are those who insist that Henry's emblem was the blue speedwell, but in the margin of a manuscript copied in his reign, I was once much struck by a long border of forget-me-nots, and I suspect that this emblem had been chosen to suit the king's new fashion. The plant we now mass for spring gardening is not quite the one the king would have used: the water forget-me-not, a similar flower with smooth stem, is often shown in early flower books under the correct French name.

Henry, however, was only the beginning, and the sequel makes his fashion seem only an example of English reserve. Three hundred and fifty years later, when men were searching their romantic souls and arguing that only wild feelings were genuine, the forget-me-not had made a home by the banks of the Danube. Splashed by the river's current it spread by the thousand into a sea of uninterrupted blue.

There were many romantic oak trees, of course, moss and a recognized corner where lovers could tie up their horses. A young couple, said a suitable romantic legend, came for a walk there at a great moment in their lives; they were due to be married next day and things were already not going too well. She was telling him that marriages last briefly, and she was not sure that brevity was right for her; she would rather call it off.

As he protested, they both saw a forget-me-not being swept downstream on the Danube's current. She took it as such women will, reasoning from one case to a general truth, and remarked that marriage was as swiftly and easily swept away as one blue flower. How wrong you are, her intended answered, and to prove it he dived into the river and saved the flower with which she had diverted the argument. But the current caught him, too, and away he was swept to his death by drowning, calling all the while 'Forget me not' to the lady he left on the bank.

The name, thereafter, stuck, and poets have made much play with this soulful German story. All very dramatic, you might think, but when you mass forget-me-nots for next spring, remembering to sow their seed as soon as possible and certainly before June begins. They must have time to build up strength for their following spring of flower.

Well-manured ground, the choice of a dark blue form, not the paler sky-blue which seeds so freely, and a corner in half-sunlight will put you well on the way to a sentimental scheme of your own. But do please sow them early in the summer, preferably as soon as their parents have finished flowering. The plants are then so much stronger for the following spring. Whether or not

Above: *Saxifraga* 'Cranbourne'. Flowers February–March. 3 ft high. Requires semi-shade, not excessively dry. In rich gritty soil is excellent. Likes lime. Easy, and will root from cuttings but they are fiddly things to take, let alone to root

Below: *Viburnum tomentosum Mariesii.* Flowers May, up to 5 ft × 10 ft wide. Loves chalk or lime. No pruning; smothers weeds eventually. A bit slow at first; not worth an amateur's while to propagate, though cuttings and layers will root

Previous page: *Myosotis* Blue Ball, Forget-me-nots. Remember to sow promptly in May for following season. Only lasts for one flowering season. Home-grown seed varies in colour, pale blue predominating

he or she then forgets you, a mass of these flowers is one of the simplest plantings that can give a gardener the sentiment he needs.

Looking at my gravel paths, I feel they could be usefully turned into a garden. Every spring they do their best to sprout seedlings for the coming summer, whereupon I do my best to stop them by soaking them in sodium chlorate; the wind blows the weedkiller on to the lawn, while unpredictable showers wash the remainder where I do not want it. By mid-June the paths are sprouting all over again, and I have to repeat the ritual. But if plants are so determined to seed themselves into gravel, why not let them do it?

I can imagine a gravel path looking pretty, unusual and healthy. Having spent many hours trying to persuade high alpine plants to flourish in England's low altitudes, I have a hunch that gravel might be, in many cases, a neat way round their difficulties.

Mixed liberally into the soil, gravel aids the drainage and keeps down the level of food, a restriction which can often cause alpine carpeters and clump-formers to put their energies into flowers rather than leaves. Suppose you like growing a small pale primrose wallflower called *Erysimum* Moonshine, as I am sure you would if you tried it. Its 4-inch-high heads of flowers would appear much more freely in the sparse diet of a gravel path than in the richer ground of a flowerbed, where it is liable to grow too fat and flower itself to death.

Or suppose you took a fancy to the many plants with silver leaves. If these were planted in a gravel bed, with gravel snugly round their necks, the dangers of rain and rotting damp in winter would decrease. There is nothing like a dose of grit and gravel for giving a plant sharp drainage. In nature, of course, it is an obvious accompaniment to plant life on a mountain. When the last spring snows are melting high on the Dolomites, the more particular sorts of cushion-plant, the androsaces and drabas and rare saxifrages, are saved from being swamped by the abundance of grit and chippings around and beneath them, through which this sudden spate of water drains safely away.

Intense mountain sun and quickly draining rainwater are the rare combination which alpine gardeners are struggling to repeat in the foggy and damp climate of a lowland garden. Gravel, at least, is one ingredient we can distribute generously. A surfacing on a flowerbed does help to stop the moisture evaporating, while handfuls underground help those frightful summer storms and winter fogs to drain away.

At this point I seem to be hovering between gravel paths and gravel gardens. The difference, I suggest, should be more one of planting than of planning. In the path I would sow or set the many free-seeding rock plants which do not mind being walked on from time to time, though heavy and continuous trampling in nailed boots is, of course, more than any carpet-plant will stand. I am thinking of thymes, soapwort, sandwort, the very smallest cotoneasters, sun rose, mints, bugle, golden marjoram, Creeping

Jenny, and generous sweeps of self-sown erinus, that most prolific of 3-inch-high tuft-like plants, which brightens up any wall or paved garden in late May with its small spikes of rose-red flowers.

I would not mind if passers-by trod several of these plants to death. Every year, I would broadcast annual seeds from a packet and hope that patches would come up to give summer colour. Toad-flax, small primrose eschscholtzias, the glorious blue phacelia, night-scented stocks and mignonette would be more than able to cope with this treatment. Seeds and gravel go surprisingly well together. I have long been watching how a group of hellebores which overhang a gravel path have seeded themselves abundantly into the gravel but not into the flowerbed. Even a hebe, some lavender and spring crocus have done the same, as have the wall-plants on the wall above. The seedlings survive in sheer gravel, shaded, admittedly, but with scarcely a trace of earth. I am sure that they would do the same where I wanted them. So, no doubt, would the weeds, and I admit that it would not be easy to plant up a gravel path in places and then soak it with weed-killer. A good selective brand would make some impression, but gardening is seldom very easy when it is trying to be different.

A gravel garden I could see more as a small yard or sunken terrace. Here, passers-by could be asked to tread especially care-fully, so that planting could be more adventurous. In the path, I would already have set bold yuccas to give a pointed shape at emphatic points in a garden surfaced with gravel. I would add acanthus, black-leaved fennel, the thistle-like eryngiums and yards of glaucous-leaved sea kale, which stays so neat in poor soil, as on its native coastlines, and gives freely of its honeyed flowers.

In between these emphatic clumps I would scatter the smallest wild geraniums, their close relations the erodiums, any amount of silver leaves, especially the smaller artemisias, campanulas galore, hebe and, for future benefit, mounds of the silver varie-gated box, perhaps the most aristocratic of all silver-marked shrubs. Anyway, you catch the idea from these suggestions.

The gravel, I think, would be the smaller pea-sized variety, mixed with half its weight of sand and a very small proportion of rich earth and leaf-mould, about four-fifths gravel and one-fifth earth. I should spread this to a depth of a foot below the path's usual surface, and water well after planting. It might turn out to be a savage starvation of plants that deserve better of their gardener. But knowing gravel, so quick to drain but convenient to preserve, I believe that plants would take it, as I have, to their heart.

Up come the weeds in the middle of May, and at once we all want them out of the way. It is surprising where they all come from: the sudden appearance of the 2-foot-high caper spurge, a visitor which is easily recognized by the thin, whitish line down its dark olive-green leaves, never ceases to amuse me. It is easily rooted out but causes dismay among many gardeners who have never seen it anywhere before.

Though sceptical of much that is now called ground-cover and though reluctant to live with the crowded and unrestful mood of a ground-cover garden, I am becoming very fond of wide-spreading shrubs. Those with horizontal branches do not seem to me to have had their full recognition, and as the new weed season races away, it is worth laying more of a plan to acquire them. Their branches do help to keep down weeds if planted in soil that begins by being fresh, because it has been cleaned with a hormone weed-killer. They also give a new line to a planting, allowing another of those contrasts which every garden needs.

Far the most easily accommodated seems to be a newish sort of laurel called *Prunus* Otto Luykens. I hate the appearance of its spotted yellow relations, but this one has dark green leaves which shine enough to reflect light. It fans them out on flat horizontal branches, reminding me of a bird which is fanning out its wings on the ground to protect its nest. It only reaches a height of 3 feet. It is evergreen, of course, though that means it sheds a few leaves in spring; it also flowers, bearing short spikes of white flowers in spring, which are pleasing but not sensational. Suppose you have wide steps in the garden, perhaps descending from an open gravel space or terrace to sit out on: one or two of these laurels planted beside the top of the steps would be most emphatic, especially if contrasted with an upright spiky shape, like a yucca or two, so splendid in town gardens, or the admirable *Phormium tenax* for southern and slightly sheltered gardens. The phormium's variegated form is particularly desirable. Horizontal laurel against vertical flax is an elementary sort of contrast, but I have never seen it tried. Those with space might try a prunus variety called *zabeliana*, which is a foot or so higher and somewhat wider. I have not yet seen it, but I imagine it is as good as the other and will likewise grow in half-shade. By laurel, incidentally, I mean the so-called cherry laurel, for the name in England now covers so many related families.

Less sombre and perhaps more magnificent is that king of all horizontal shrubs for chalk gardens, *Viburnum plicatum tomentosum*, either Lanarth variety or *mariesii*. This loses its leaves in winter but brings late May to life with a massive display of white flowers, born flat on upright individual stems along horizontal branches. It is an original shrub which owners of wide spaces must consider before any other deciduous plant. It often turns a vivid colour in autumn and in some Octobers it bears red berries, like its relation the compact Guelder rose. I do not know why the berries occur in some years, not others, but you must be patient, no less than with the deceptively small specimen your nurseryman will send you. After five or six years you will be well on the way to a big shrub, some 8 feet tall and perhaps 12 feet wide. It will stand boldly in rough grass, but I would like to underplant it with the fashionably grey *Senecio laxifolius*, an infallibly easy shrub in sunshine, where it makes large low mounds for those who wisely trim it back and pinch out the tips of its shoots in late April.

Phormium tenax, New Zealand Flax. Leaves up to 4 ft, flowers negligible, and unpredictable except in wild areas. Hardy against a south wall; not always reliable inland. Propagation is difficult

A flower which is painted in the foreground of Botticelli's *Birth of Venus*, a flower from which Britain itself was once believed to take its name: if anybody ever offered you the plant behind this evocative history, I hope you would welcome it into the garden even if it ran about like bindweed and looked only slightly less ugly than edelweiss. In fact, ugly is the last thing you could call it and despite its stirring history, it is in no way a rarity, although surprisingly few gardeners grow or know it now. It is none other than old *Rosa alba* in all its many delightful forms.

Rose alba is, of course, the old white rose of York. It has the strongest possible claim to be the national emblem of all England too: the Roman Pliny in the first century AD mentioned that Britannia was also known as Albion and explained its second name by the masses of white roses known to grow there. As *alba* is the Latin for 'white', it was not a stupid guess. It is very possible that what we now call *Rosa alba* was the rose he meant. Certainly there are many old bushes of it still growing wild in this country, particularly, I believe, in Cheshire. In my opinion, there ought to be many more in captivity in the garden.

The great merit of all its varieties is that they are extraordinarily tough. I have never seen *Rosa alba* with disease and if, like me, you prefer the old roses to the latest cracking scarlets from the flori-bunda breeders, you will know how valuable that is.

Many of the most luscious old Bourbons, Hybrid Perpetuals and so forth suffer recurrently from black spot or mildew and only nostalgia still induces me to try them. But *alba* is different. It even thrives in semi-shade or, better still, against a cold north wall. I have seen it as a wonderful summer hedge or even as a bush, centuries old, fighting its way into flower among a wilderness of weeds. There is much good sense in growing the plants that are known to like this country.

The most beautiful form is *alba* Celestial, one of those roses which looks its best when still in bud. It is the most remarkable shell-pink, very pure even when the small double flowers are open. It grows into an elegant shape, upright and with branches of exquisite silver-grey foliage which go so well with every shade of pale pink. 'Ah,' say the sceptics and the lovers of hybrid teas, 'but it only flowers once'. Maybe, but so do magnolias and it would be a good thing if roses as strident as Super Star or Masquerade were restricted to one short burst too. Better to have beauty once than harshness all the summer.

Queen of Denmark runs Celestial very close. Its fault is its straggliness, but if these *alba* roses are pruned very hard in late December, this can be overcome. Its flowers are luxuriant, darker pink at the centre and paler at the outside but always heavy with ruffled petals, the sort of colour you get if you mash up raspberries with plenty of cream. The leaves are grey-green and look excel-lent if the bush is trained against a wall.

Two close relations have the same range of colouring, though not, like Queen of Denmark, all at once in one flower. Felicité

Rosa banksiae lutea. Climber, very tall. Hardy on south walls, but scarcely so inland. Needs much sun and warmth for best flowering. I am not sure how to prune it most wisely. Probably thin it lightly after flowering

June

70

Parmentier is cream when in bud, double white when first open and pale pink when ageing and about to fade. Its smaller flowers have the best form when fully developed of any *alba* and I would like to see it in a long bed below a wall with hostas or dark blue lavender Hidcote in front for contrast.

Great Maiden's Blush, however, is a little bigger though it passes through the same colour range: the French call it Aroused Maiden's Thigh, untranslatably, and Vita Sackville-West adored it. It does have all the freshness of its name and no old rose enthusiast should omit it.

These later varieties are not the plant which Pliny knew or which Botticelli or Giotto decided to paint: the nearest to that is *alba maxima*, a taller bush with double pure-white flowers which are just as charming as their history. The semi-double *semi-plena* is well worth growing too, for it has a very distinguished air. The story goes that this was the rose which Flora Macdonald gave as a farewell present to Bonnie Prince Charlie. Certainly, it is still very often seen in Scotland and the story may well be true.

It goes without saying that all those old *albas* smell delicious, especially if they are planted in the sun. For three weeks in June you can revel in their scent of honey and spices for very little trouble indeed. Six hundred years ago, a gardening monk remarked that this white rose made bushes with trunks many times thicker than a man's arm. Cultivation has improved since then and though the weather may be worse, they should do even better in your gardens.

Some time ago, I was amusing myself with that baffling problem: when is a plant not an animal? Superficially, it sounds quite simple: we all have a clear mental picture of a plant, green-leaved, sprouting, rooted and sometimes flowering. But mental pictures are never enough. Some plants are not green-leaved, some do not sprout, others do not root, many do not 'flower' and some even prefer to eat meat. I am not a botanist and I know no scientific definitions: if I did, I would not use muddling terms like flower or root, as they are conveniences which hide some terrible confusions.

The more I thought, the more complicated my problem became. I sympathized with those Elizabethans who classed the garden mandrake as a living animal or with John Parkinson who included a unicorn's horn in his herbal encyclopaedia. Was my garden really a zoo? There is a squishy thing called *Euglaena* which muddles even the botanists as it feeds through its cell walls, the mark of a plant, while moving about, the mark of an animal.

At first thought this difference in movement seemed reassuring. Unlike a herd of zebra, my winter irises would not move elsewhere as soon as my back was turned. But reassurance was short-lived; is not growth a form of spontaneous movement and are not plants the natural travellers of the world? This led me back to a less perplexing tangle: how plants, like animals, have spread or travelled and how man has helped them on his way. The more one thinks about this, the more human the plants become.

Rosa mundi. Up to 4 ft. Flowers July, once only. Worth pruning to base immediately after flowering. Cuttings will root then quite easily

73

First, these travellers' background. Gardeners forget what a scramble for position goes on beneath their flowerbeds. Experts have calculated that one single birch tree will produce about seven hundred thousand nuts with wings. Yet only one of these must germinate to keep the birch population constant. It is imperative, therefore, that annually they fall on stony or unsuitable ground: 'many are called but few are chosen' is the practical moral to the parable of the sower. The birch is only one example; chickweed, groundsel or a puffball fungus are horrifyingly prolific, while family planning among foxgloves would be a hopelessly lost cause.

For each plant, then, which grows there are millions which do not. But with millions going spare, movement and travel are inevitable. This is where man and the animals come in. When Darwin trapped a red-legged partridge and saved the ball of mud clinging to its leg, he germinated more than eighty seedlings from the earth he saved. Bird messes produced similar results.

But plants are not always the passive victim. Butterworts, sundews, goosegrass or tumbleweed are catchers and clingers, sticking and hooking themselves on to passing animals and hitching a lift elsewhere. Willow-herb and balsams are catapulted. Gummed to man's boots or to his tractor wheels, the pineapple weed has spread itself all over the country. Yet it only arrived from America a hundred years ago.

The more man interferes with his surroundings, the more the conditions of plant movement change. Interference can be a blessing: if elder bushes were left to their own devices, they would soon choke the course of valuable streams. Interference can also give eager travellers their chance: ragwort and rose-bay willow herb revelled in the rubble of a bombed-out site.

The bomb-crater on Box Hill near Dorking, I read recently, was a case in point. Within six months, its freshly turned soil had sprouted foxgloves and thirty different kinds of foreign plants, mainly European, so that men suspected a chance addition to the bomb itself, a sort of botanical broadside from the Ruhr. This implausibe theory was widely believed until a man admitted that he had sown the seeds from packets while out on a walk because he thought the crater needed cheering up. His interference infuriated field botanists who had been keeping their records of 'native' plants as pure as possible. But botanists apart, his idea was sympathetic. It was not, however, very practical. Such is the ferocious scramble of nature that foreign seeds will often fail. His sowing has now been swamped by hazels.

But sometimes a defenceless foreigner has had the last laugh. The blue speedwell, *Veronica filiformis,* arrived here by 1770, having been collected from its native Caucasus. It sets seed very seldom and can only travel by root. It faced a land where speedwells were already established, where every inch of soil was being fought over by countless surplus seeds, and yet by 1950 it was spread all over the British Isles, revelling in Ireland and only faltering in very dry soil. Wherever a scrap of root touched the earth, it flourished, and at first gardener passed it to gardener as a useful alpine plant.

Once they discovered its rampageous nature they passed it despairingly to friends. When there were few ignorant friends left, they slung it on to rubbish heaps. From rubbish heaps, it crept to hedges and roadsides, where it now sits, mocking the farmer and the passer-by.

The most human story of all, however, belongs to the London ragwort. This weed is a hybrid child of two exuberant parents, one of which is the squalid or Oxford ragwort, whose story begins in the seventeenth century, when it was sent from its home on Mount Etna to the Oxford Botanic Gardens. By the nineteenth century, its prolific seeds had blown far and wide round the city. Then came the Great Western Railway. The trains created a rushing draught, the tracks supplied congenial pebbles and the ragwort raced on a one-way ticket to Paddington as its seeds blew down between the sleepers. It arrived in time for the Second World War, waited till bombs had piled up the rubble and then moved into the new open spaces.

Meanwhile, our own sticky groundsel had done likewise from its home on the Southern Region. Thriving on bomb sites, the two met, married and produced a hybrid child, *Senecio londinensis* or the rare London ragwort; as a penalty for its parents' morals, the London ragwort is sterile.

A Sicilian arriving in Oxford and taking the town by storm, catching the railway to London in time for a bomb-site romance with a British war refugee, the sexual sins of the parents being visited on a blameless son: this strange succession of circumstances is worthy of any modern novel. Why plants are not animals I still cannot decide. But in their travels, they have behaved in alarmingly human ways.

'Scents are the souls of flowers: they may even be perceptible in the world of shadows.' Philosophically, this is a fantasy with little to recommend it: it is no surprise to find it was written by an aged Frenchman. In a gardener, however, logic is seldom a virtue, and I would like to believe that the Frenchman had right on his side, for scents are indeed the very essence of the garden. It would also mean that all the orange blossoms now in flower are destined for immortality.

Orange blossom (or *Philadelphus*) is the shrub which I could least do without. It grows fast and smells glorious. All the different varieties have those lovely white flowers. Wherever it is, it forces its presence on us: one small gust of wind and that scent of juicy tangerines, not oranges, is spread for yards around. At night it is almost luminous in its whiteness and among trees or semi-shaded woods it is a surprise that never fails to swamp a visitor's senses.

The only problem is its name (which it cannot help): the old still try and call it *Syringa* which, of course, is the proper name for lilac, whereas the experts know it as *Philadelphus*. In Greek, the

latter means 'fondness for one's brother', a name so appropriate for this friendly plant that we should gladly put up with occasional confusion. *Philadelphus coronarius* was grown in Elizabethan times and I still think it is among the best. It has four points in its favour: its creamy flowers are small, they are produced earlier than most other sorts; their smell is not too sickly and is retained even when the flowers are well faded. This last virtue makes it a wise and unusual choice for pot-pourri. It was very widely grown in Italy in the seventeenth century but there seem to be few traces of it there nowadays. It is extremely easy to grow in sun or shade and can often reach a height of 10 feet. From it has come a new hybrid, *zeyheri,* which is pure white and not very much of an improvement.

Coronarius, I feel, is at its best when allowed to run wild, but not every garden has room to let it have its way. Instead, there is a golden-leaved form *coronarius aureus,* which grows far more slowly. It is certainly very striking when in leaf but has many fewer flowers and therefore is rather a disappointment. It can be curiously difficult to grow well and I think it thrives and looks its best in semi-shade, unlike many golden-leaved plants. There it can be massed to give a clump of fresh leaves in early summer, 3 or 4 feet high and scented from the inconspicuous white flowers up its stems. A much better specimen shrub would be Beauclerk, which grows in an arching manner and has masses of wide-petalled flowers of pure white; it begins to flower as *coronarius* finishes. Eventually it is 7 feet high and every year covers itself in those sweet flowers, the mark of an excellent modern variety.

Good as Beauclerk is, Virginal is even better, as it is more upright, needs less room to spread and also has ruffled double flowers. If I had to choose one orange blossom for a garden, this would be it. One nursery catalogue has rudely discontinued it 'because the newer Enchantment is so much better'. I have never seen this to be so; Virginal is a little leggy but it is smothered in flower and has the good contrast of a dark green leaf. Again, its scent is heavy; if you prefer the smell of pineapples to tangerines you would, however, be happier with either Belle Etoile or the very free-flowering *lemoinei erectus.* Both are, sadly, single flowered, though Belle Etoile has the compensation of a purple blotch in the centre of each flower.

Ideally, I would plan these orange blossoms for continuity: a splash of *coronarius* for early June, then *lemoinei* and Virginal and finally, Beauclerk and the tall, single *burfordiensis* with its chalice-shaped flowers which sometimes last till the third week in July. I always think how glorious they would be massed in hedges either side of a rough-mown walk, with a statue, perhaps, at the end: the only pity is that none is evergreen, and therefore they lack the firm shape for a mass in a formal garden near a house.

All this sounds rather grand but there are smaller philadelphus too. Manteau d'Hermine is the smallest, merely 3 feet high and wide with very small double flowers early in June. To follow on,

Philadelphus coronarius, smaller flowered variety. Easily rooted from July cuttings. Prune after flowering

comes Silver Showers, an admirable 4-foot shrub whose surprisingly large single flowers are shaped like a cup. These two plants mean that even the smallest garden has room for a continuity of orange blossom: each smells very good. I would like to try them in a big hole in paving stones with a seat nearby from which I could enjoy their wafting scent. And there I could sit and wonder whether, after all, that scent is not so strong that it will indeed be perceptible in the world of shadows too. For the next world, the Greeks promised us meadows of that dingy asphodel, the Romans agreed and Christianity confined its flowers to members of Paradise only. How nice it would be if Monsieur Joubert were right and smells like the scent of orange blossom did await us all.

This is a suggestion for those who like their food. It is not, however, for those who judge what they eat in terms of quantity, as the fruits I want to recommend are not a dish to make you feel full. Everybody knows the big fat strawberries of June but it is their small alpine relations which I strongly urge you to try.

First, their merits. They bear fruit almost continuously from June to October and they are the least fussy delicacy to grow. Unlike inflated varieties, Royal Sovereign and others, they need no nets and none of those ugly layers of straw which protect ordinary strawberries from birds or wet earth.

For me that is a great blessing. One year, we tried to festoon our strawberry bed with a skein of much-publicized nylon thread, and as a result every strawberry we picked brought a train of wispy white 'wool' with it. Nylon, I fear, is not on its best behaviour in a gusty spring wind. So as far as conventional strawberries go, that was – forgive me – the last straw.

But alpine strawberries need no protection; those chattering blackbirds are too stupid to realize how well they taste. As they carry their small fruits on upright wiry stems as much as one foot above the ground, there is no danger that they will rot on the earth. They are easier to pick as you do not have to rummage for them in the leaves. I have never known them catch a disease and nowadays that is a rare recommendation for a strawberry. They need two encouragements: plenty of water, as much as a hosing every day in spring and summer, and plenty of well-rotted manure, especially on light ground. If they are thirsty or starved, they will not fruit properly. I cannot blame them for that.

So much for my panegyric: now, the drawbacks. To enjoy a good helping for four, you need rather a lot of plants. Do not think of their crop in terms of weight: half a pound of their nut-like fruit goes a very long way. But each individual berry is about the size of those old silver threepenny bits, so you must pick plenty in order to make a meal. The trouble is that they are expensive. Abroad, you often find varieties which spread by runners and, of course, those are easy to increase for yourselves.

But in England, the one easily available variety is Baron Solemacher and excellent though he is, he does not make easily detachable layers. With these small strawberries, you must think in multiples of 100, and if you buy growing plants, each 100 costs £12 or more. What the nurserymen tend to forget is that alpine strawberries are a short-term investment, as the plants are past their best after two years. However, if you feel rich, lazy and tempted, I recommend the improved strain offered handily in pots by the Broadwell Nursey, Broadwell, Moreton-in-the-Marsh, Glos. Being pot grown, they can be bought at any season.

For the less rich, there are compensations. I recently discovered that seed is the answer to the problem. Sow it in boxes in September and prick out the seedlings next month, wintering them preferably in a cold frame or greenhouse. Plant them out in their bed in early April leaving about 15 inches between each plant and about 3 feet between rows. Miraculously, they fruit well in their first year, but by their third they will need replacing. Their seed is very fine, so dust a little sand over the top and do not bury it in earth. I do not advise you to water the boxes until the seeds have come up. From two or three packets you should raise hundreds.

My other warning is, naturally, that they do not taste like proper strawberries. They are not an acquired taste, like cigarettes or whisky; either you like their pungent stickiness or you do not. Soak them in plenty of caster sugar overnight before eating. Do not spoil them with cream but give them a dash of sweet white wine and serve them in tall glasses. I am sorry that sounds so house-and-garden, but it is an excellent recipe. Alpine strawberry jam is a luxury second only to alpine strawberries mixed with blueberries and flavoured with lemon.

In an age obsessed with covering gardens' ground, a job which I often prefer to leave to the much-maligned weeds, alpine strawberries should be fashionable. As in their native woods, they are happy in light shade provided that they are watered well. Beneath fruit trees in a cottage garden they will grow into a low carpet which would be welcome without any flowers or berries. Never be afraid to mix the many beautiful fruits and vegetables in among your flowers. Much of modern gardening is a battle against the artificial divisions of rose, shrub, herbaceous, fruit and vegetable gardens: all are plants and plants belong in profusion together. From June to October, alpine strawberries can be enjoyed in a quiet way: that is more than can be said for dahlias, chrysanthemums, asters and the other set pieces of an autumn flower garden.

This is the time of year when I wish I could have camellias in the garden. They are out of flower, of course, but at the start of June, I look back over notes made during the spring and every year their name is high among them. They have such glistening green leaves that they reflect the light in any half-shaded garden. That is why I prefer them to most rhododendrons, whose matt leaves drain a place of any light and atmosphere.

Those long debates about the rhododendron being foreign, and therefore unsuited to the British landscape, seem to me to miss most of the point. Roses and camellias are foreign or man-made

too, and nobody wants to ban them. It is all a question of appearance. Light is a prime quality in the look of a garden plant. The leaves of many roses catch the light unusually, whereas those of most rhododendrons do not. It is time we paid attention to the light in our rose leaves as much as to the glare in their flowers.

Granted that camellias glisten, I have never had suitably lime-free earth in which to enjoy them. The water supply is equally limy, and to keep camellias happy in tubs would require rain water, with which I cannot be bothered. Treatment with the chemical Sequestrene makes available the trace elements lost to some plants in limy soil, but it is not cheap and it is always demanding. A wiser method is to dig out a 3-foot-deep hole, line it with a double thickness of polythene sheeting and fill this with peat and leaf mould. The sheet keeps the peat and the plant's roots away from the lime outside. It is quite an effort, so I have let the camellia be and have planted pinks instead. The camellia, unlike the pink, can be enjoyed second-hand through the memory of a delightful history.

Those who know their operas will not need reminding of the young Violetta, the Lady of the Camellias, in Verdi's *La Traviata*. Drawn from a novel by Dumas, she was also, to Dumas, a real person.

A French country girl came to Paris in the 1840s at the age of fifteen, took a job in a dressmaker's shop and found herself stitching seams for the dresses of musicians' girlfriends. One musician, Liszt no less, came in person to collect his presents from the dress-

Above: *Camellia japonica* Western Rose

Right: *Philadelphus* Belle Etoile, Orange Blossom. June, arching branches to 6 ft. Any soil, sun or semi-shade. Never prune in the spring; best trimmed in July, if at all. Easily rooted from July cuttings. Exquisite scent

Overleaf: Rose Queen of Denmark. A tough alba rose, to 6 ft. June flowering only. Will grow on a north wall. Cuttings will root. Best in July

80

shop. Arriving at one of the many neurotic moments in his life, he was much taken with the country seamstress, who promptly fell in love with him. He took her out, she met a wide range of artists and started an affair with the younger Dumas. All society wanted to meet her, for the desire for variety is nothing new in the public's private life. The name of Alphonsine Plessin became famous among the girls of Paris. She was easily distinguished as the girl who always wore a white camellia.

The camellia was a fashionable choice. We know how the Dutch went mad for tulips in the seventeenth century, but just when Dumas had written *The Black Tulip,* Paris was bidding madly for the newer range of the camellias. Alphonsine the dressmaker led the way and when she died at the age of twenty-two, the Parisian cult of the camellia had the necessary spark of sentiment to touch it off. Her coffin was filled with white camellias; her countless admirers wore the flower in their buttonholes; the Dutch saw a market and started to exploit it. If the French were still strewing camellias on a dressmaker's Montmartre grave, the demand for the flower should be as big as salesmen could make it.

Rising to the opportunity, the Dutch decided to hold lotteries. The English gave them the raw materials, charging thousands of guilders to ship the first red and white striped camellia from Bromley, where it had recently been raised. It was called Queen Victoria and its cuttings could be bought for a 200-franc ticket: Paris rushed in to buy it and within six months the lottery had raised 20,000 francs. The plant was sold from country to country, raffled again and made to yield twice as much. Three years later a Queen Victoria cost only three francs and several green fingers had been badly burned.

Paris could still not leave her favourite flower alone. Twenty-five years later, a rich fancier hoped to repeat the performance. He ordered two newly-bred varieties to be shipped across from New Orleans in a protective bed of moss at vast expense. Foolishly, he bought them only from the prospectus; they arrived, not worth their description, and after two ineffective court cases, he staged his way out of embarrassment.

The two disputed bushes, he announced, would be shown in the Champs Elysées for the French public to decide their value. The entrance fee was nominal, a band played themes from *La Traviata* and such was the crowd of visitors that the demand caused the ticket's price to double. Flowers from the American camellias were sold for thousands of francs apiece. That night, some had found their way to Alphonsine's Montmartre grave. Two years later, the plant could be bought for a song.

Those of you who garden on acid soil will not need reminding that men would once give anything for one camellia. It is never too troublesome to give it space and to cover it in March with a cage of nylon netting. This string vest takes the edge off the damaging spring frosts by an insulating pocket of air. Otherwise, the buds are often browned before they open.

Camellia Donation

85

Except for the pointed stake, the use of the motor mower or the wonky ladder, gardening is a relaxation, a pleasure which is a challenge without ever becoming a risk. It has little to offer to those in search of danger, yet nothing is more satisfying than a well-grown garden in midsummer with flowers to delight the senses and the problem of why we enjoy them to occupy the brain.

Beside me now, there stands a clump of white July lilies, *Lilium regale*. Overwhelmed by their powerful scent and the purple outsides of their trumpet flowers, today, at least, I vote them to be my favourite flower. Nothing could be more peaceful and nowadays *regale* lilies are old familiar friends. But it was not always so. Behind their innocent white flowers stretches a tale of high drama. What I am now enjoying derives from one man's bravery in the face of extreme danger.

A *regale* lily looks as though it has been in our garden for centuries. In fact, it was not discovered until 1910. In that year, Mr Ernest Wilson, the noted plant collector from Chipping Camden, had been sponsored by Americans to return to China, the happiest of hunting grounds for enterprising botanists of the day. He headed for the Min Valley, on the borders of Tibet, an ignored area known only from native rumours. One midday, descending into the river gorge, he was met by a sight which has guaranteed his gardening reputation. All over the banks of the precipice grew *Lilium regale,* as we now know it.

'Surrounded by mountains of shale and granite,' he later wrote, 'whose peaks are clothed with eternal snow, the *regale* lily has its home, not in twos or fives, but in hundreds, in thousands – yes, in tens of thousands.'

From the sedan chair in which he always travelled he sent his Chinese coolies to collect the bulbs as abundantly as they could. Thousands were dug up until, ominously, the shale began to slip and the rockface slipped forward in an avalanche. Over went the sedan and Wilson was crushed by a boulder on his leg, his men having scattered in horror.

There he lay for hours till his servants returned to his rescue. Prising him free, they stretched him on the road and inspected the damage. While they did so, a train of local mules ran by; Wilson was in no condition to be moved. The only road was so narrow that he had blocked it, and all fifty anumals clattered over his body in order to get past before the avalanche began again. Despite the shock of their hooves passing inches above him, he clung on to the remaining bulbs, determined to bring them to safety.

Ingeniously, he set his leg in the remains of his camera tripod and, though seriously ill, was hoisted on to his bearers' shoulders to be carried for three days back to base. There the leg festered and was nearly amputated, but the lily bulbs, some six thousand, were shipped at once to Boston. Wilson recovered and was fit enough to walk for another twenty years, but his valley has never been revisited since. From that original stock all the *regale* lilies in our gardens are now grown.

July

Few bulbs have been so harrowing to collect, but no lily is so delightfully easy to grow. For any garden, big or small, it is essential. In a town, if space is short, it can easily be planted in pots, three to a width of 7 inches, and put outside on pavings or terraces. It needs a covering of 4 inches of soil above the top of the bulb; a top inch or so of mulch is a good idea and it does not mind lime.

Its home, as described by Wilson, explains its toughness; terrific heat in summer with sudden thunderstorms too violent for man or beast. In recent dry spells it has been disappointing, growing shorter and flowering very briefly. Obviously, lack of water is to blame. Like most lilies it is happiest when sited with other plants around its roots. Its 4-foot stems look especially fine when emerging from silver leaves. Try planting a grey artemisia like *splendens* or *discolor* above it and allowing it to come through them each year. They stop it looking naked and are an excellent foil to the flowers, wine-purple outside, white inside, with yellow middles.

Its blessing, however, is the ease with which it grows from seed, a fitting justice after the troubles of introducing the originals. You can easily collect your own when ripe in August and then sow them at once, preferably in some heat. By late September the seedlings should be transplanted 6 inches apart in open ground. They may well flower in their second year and certainly thereafter. By sowing a little seed each year you can build up a big succession for no cost at all. Now that a full-grown bulb costs 40p or more there is much to be said for patience. Like every lily, *regale* moves best in the autumn and not when dry in spring, for no lily bulb is ever dormant. But unless you grow your own, no nursery will supply you with them when they are still in leaf.

On a summer's evening this lily is the most soothing of flowers with a scent that uplifts the gloomiest corner of the garden. Its loveliness is an added reason for remembering Ernest Wilson; peaceful though a garden is, it too has been bettered by the efforts of brave men.

Lavender is a plant which everybody knows and many people grow but its popularity has never made it common. It is as well to remember that this can be so, as gardeners tend to divide themselves into two groups—those who only grow what they see repeatedly in other gardens (the motor car has had some influence here, as it has made it possible to look out of the window at nothing but forsythia and floribunda roses) and those who only grow what others will find difficult to recognize.

The snobs look down on the copycats; the copycats in turn become aggressive in defence of their marigolds and on at least two occasions in the past six months, I have known old friends become quarrelsome about the relative merits of stocks and sarcococcas. As often, each side has firm hold of one part of the truth but they are convinced that the part which they hold is really the whole. Yet there are plants to bridge their differences, none more appropriate than the lavender bush, familiar, often

planted, but still a choice for the connoisseur.

Lavender is a plant with a long and respectable history, spreading from the Mediterranean to the medieval gardens of the monks, and from monasteries to the formal parterres of the seventeenth century; the white variety was much favoured by Henrietta Maria, the 'blue' by Miss Gertrude Jekyll, most perceptive of garden planters in the Edwardian age.

This Mediterranean origin suggests its use in the garden. Lavender is a plant for an aromatic border, breathing the smells of last year's summer holiday; in a small garden, many plant drifts of lavender along the path to the house. Beneath the house I would mix the less common varieties with aromatic cistus and the pungent helichrysum, tucking in a few golden marjorams and lemon-scented thyme (called *citriodorus)* to spill forwards over the path. A daphne for spring, either the Somerset variety or the sweet *odora aureo marginata,* the wide-spreading, golden-leaved hardy *Fuschia* Graf de Wit for autumn, and I would have a planting to be enjoyed throughout the year. The winter iris (called *unguicularis)* could be added beneath a south wall to brighten the heart in January.

I value lavender so highly because of its freedom of flower, range of colouring and gentleness of outline. There are those who complain that for three-quarters of the year it looks spiky and awkward but this is a view which I do not share; the different varieties must all be used differently and only in the wrong place do their faults become too obvious. But all lavenders do have one maddening habit against which you must be warned; after six years, they begin to grow leggy or catch a disease which makes them die out in bits and pieces, leaving a healthy branch or two to encourage you to spare them for another season.

A hard trimming after the bushes have flowered can help to delay the degeneration but even so, you can only look on lavender as a short-lived feature. As soon as they become patchy, throw them out. When planting their bushes on heavy clay soils I always dig in a liberal dose of sand, as lavender, native of the seaside, thrives in the lightest earth. But even on sand, cuttings must be kept to replace the middle-aged. Never waste money buying lavender in dozens or hundreds. Cuttings taken in April or August are absurdly easy to root, being ready for their permanent home within nine months of leaving their parent.

The way to enjoy lavender is to know the varieties to suit your purpose. For drifts between evergreen shrubs and topiary or for edgings to gravel paths, far the neatest kind is the dark lavender Hidcote, 18 inches tall, grey-green leaved and though rather desolate in winter, a very subtle picture in July when thickset with its spikes of indigo flowers, like coloured ears of wheat. The taller form called Hidcote Giant is even more magnificent, though very hard to buy nowadays.

The paler varieties called Munstead and Twickel Purple are taller, more straggly and much less emphatic; though these are

Above: *Daphne odora aureo-marginata* from close up

Below: *Iris unguicularis,* Winter Iris from Algeria. 12 in stems in January–February; happiest in more rubble than earth at foot of very sunny wall. Stems should be pulled, not picked, for vases indoors. Best transplanted in September from divisions. Can be slow to settle

the usual lavender colours, I do not think they are worth the trouble any more. Rather than the washy lavender, I patronize the greyish white, an unusual plant which gardeners have been slow to appreciate. In its smallest form, known by one nursery as Baby White, it is only 9 inches high, very slow growing and extraordinarily aromatic. Its branches are easily broken, and as soon as they are rubbed, they smell of the strongest lavender bags.

The place for this obliging plant is a hole in paving or a dry wall; there, it will spread very slowly to a width of a foot. Even after nine years, my oldest plant shows no sign of disease. This, I believe, refutes those who think lavender can only be massed for the sake of its flowers, for this small shrub is always tidy and one specimen is always welcome; its companion, Baby or Hidcote Pink, is lavender-mauve. I grow it but I do not think it is a plant for those who like value for space and money.

On a grander scale, there are two uncommon kinds for planting in ones and twos; the first is a large grey-white variety, now stocked only by John Scott Ltd, of the Royal Nurseries, Merriott, Somerset, which grows to an impressive 3 feet and looks dramatic beside a flight of steps or at the corner of a gravel path. The second is called French lavender, *Lavandula stoechas*, at most only 2 feet tall but with regimented heads of purple flowers, softened by a tuft of upturned lavender bracts, like coloured leaves. It looks rather impudent and it pays for its insolence in very severe winters by being cut to pieces by frost. I like it very much indeed and wish you would plant it and risk the frost more often.

The large white variety, too, is susceptible to the cold but at the foot of an Oxfordshire wall, both came happily through the past three winters. South of York, I feel sure they are worth a risk: by being adventurous, you can have your lavender, satisfy conservative gardeners and still intrigue the connoisseur.

I believe gardeners nowadays should only bother with the best. They need the best plants for their conditions, planted to the best design, a very important part of gardening which we should all take as seriously as dead-heading the roses. Believing in the best, I went recently to what seems likely to be the best garden in England at the best time of the year.

Sissinghurst Castle, in the Weald of Kent, has been made famous as much through the pen as the spade. Its slow accumulation of features and firm outline was described for ten years in the finest gardening articles ever written, by its creator, Vita Sackville-West. If there are still gardeners who do not know them, after the hundreds of thousands who have read them in books and newspapers and visited Sissinghurst as a result, a selection is still available under the title of *V. Sackville-West's Garden Book*, published by Michael Joseph.

Mind you, this is only a selection. But it gives you a broad avenue down which to approach the abundant alleys and secret gardens of the real Sissinghurst at its far end. This approach can be made any day between 1 April and mid-October, from midday

Sissinghurst Yew Roundel: a fine example of a simple architectural planting, in imitation of the round threshing floors on Kent Weald farms

till 6.30 p.m. on weekdays, 10 a.m. to 6.30 p.m. on weekends and Bank Holidays. The garden now belongs to the National Trust.

Walking under the first of the castle's old brick Tudor arches and watching the white pigeons flap off the lawn like a pack of cards, I was at once struck by how much of this great garden has been stolen and copied. Old-fashioned roses, white gardens, informal planting in formal design, roses up fruit trees, fruit trees in borders, broad-headed onion flowers in beds, again, of old roses: I dare say there were models for most of these ideas before Miss Sackville-West applied them, and certainly she owed much of their detail to the writings of the great Miss Jekyll. But I am sure that her writings and the success of her own garden are the reasons why they recur in other great garden plantings, from Kiftsgate to Killerton, from Cranborne to Crathes Castle.

The Sissinghurst style, with a few Versailles tubs from Sloane Street and a few of the newly-fashionable green flowers, has become the ideal of gentlemanly taste, the copse and serpentine lake to the twentieth century's Bathursts and Burlingtons. There have been few artists since Poussin who have laid down for so many what a particular sort of landscape should look like; imitators usually simplify, and the pupils of V. Sackville-West seem to me to have overlooked one necessary part of Sissinghurst.

This is not just a garden of pale restraint and civility, although it is closed to French marigolds and scarlet salvias. The cult of the pastel colour and the sensitive sweep of grey and silver seems to me as much a proof of deficient taste as the beds of gay blue lobelia and china pink asters which the country-house class disdains as too common. Most of history's civilized tastes have also turned to an exotic alternative, as a bold expression of all that their civilized ideals of restraint and balanced harmony would otherwise deny them. V. Sackville-West valued warmth and generous richness in colours of her flowers. Just as the patrons of classical Georgian houses had a taste for Oriental romances, for gipsy tales and poems set in the East, so this planter of a classically formal garden, designed with extraordinary skill by her husband Harold Nicolson, drew on the gorgeous store of the East for the comparisons and combinations which have made her garden and her writings so distinctive.

A mass of pansies seemed to her like a Persian carpet; wine-purple roses suggested damask and Isfahan: she planned for the peacock colours of the tigridia and the columbine as much as for the silver-leaved pears and the white climbing roses which others now admire. Her passion for the old roses, which she did so much to revive, was mixed with a love of Provençal sunshine, tapestry and the romantic colours of the Crusades. She would have understood that the finest roses that I have seen were not in Queen Mary's rose garden but wild, white and single-flowered in the Afghan foothills north of Kabul.

Sissinghurst is well known as a garden of compartments, of yew-hedged rooms for different seasons, privacies and firm straight lines. It is less often seen as a gay carpet of warmth and colour, though much of it was planted in order to mix and control this idea. The cottage garden of reds and yellows can be excused as only a cottage experiment, but the mixed colours of the ordinary *Aquilegia* or columbine, which we can all grow from a packet of seed, are to my mind the emblem of Sissinghurst in summer. A courtyard filled with columbines was one of Miss Sackville-West's ambitions, but it is not, perhaps, the one which many of her followers still see in her example. Under the care of the National Trust, Sissinghurst is astonishingly well gardened, so that one takes it for granted that there are no weeds, only the rarest sign of mildew on all its countless roses, and that every old rose bush is trained on stakes and pinned perfectly to walls. But there is one planting that springs first to my mind when I think the garden over, and I suspect it began with the owner. It is very simple and obliging.

Beneath a pink brick wall the dark velvet flowers of the purple-black *Pelargonium* Lord Bute shows through a group of the navy blue-purple Cherry Pie in its deepest and richest form. Beside the pair of them grows the ash-grey and pink-leaved *Fuchsia tricolor* in its tough, variegated form. This small shrub changes the shading of its leaves from pink to grey-green throughout the summer, according to the youth of its shoots and the diligence of the bugs which obligingly eat the leaves as they age and become drab. These three plants have the warm opulence which their owner loved, and the heavy scent of Cherry Pie in sunshine gives the planting an even richer tone.

Sissinghurst's white garden has perhaps made more impression on the gardening public than any other planting of the past thirty years. Even since Vita Sackville-West conceived it, survived the doubts expressed in the return post by her correspondent husband Harold Nicolson, and turned it into exactly the effect she outlined in her first note about the idea, white gardens have been very much in the night air of English country gardens. I can think of fifteen, at least, only two of which are suited to their surroundings. Such is the power of photographs and prose as entertaining as Miss Sackville-West's. I was prepared for a disappointment when I went to see the mother of them all.

Its effect is indeed astonishing and close inspection shows how art has worked and softened the original idea of whiteness. The centrepiece had once been four white almond trees, but they had died and a pleasing iron frame has now replaced and improved on them. It was smothered with the single rampant white Kiftsgate rose and a small button-flowered white companion which I suspect to have been Bobbie James.

There was scarcely as much white in the garden as silver, not only the silver of the most magnificent weeping silver-leaved pear tree (*Pyrus salicifolia pendula*, which you should place carefully if you have not yet got one) but also the silver of small *Convolvulus cneorum*, the marvellous cut-leaved *Senecio leucostachys* and the

Above: *Lilium regale:* June–July, up to 4 ft. No manure, happy on lime. Plant about 3–5 in deep. Flowers in second year from abundant seed, sown in drills outdoors when ripe

Below: *Cardiocrinum giganteum.* Flowers July. Up to 7 ft. Best in leafy soil, cool, shaded at roots but open to light. Must never dry out. Seldom survives to flower a second time. Propagation is very slow, cultivation difficult, except in some Scottish gardens

felted grey round leaves of *Helichrysum petiolatum,* both of which are excellent accompaniments to a summer border.

There were white flowers, of course, the tall white haze of the flowering sea kale, white galega, cranesbill, a white pink named after John Gray and a delphinium which in your garden could well be the huge white Swan Lake. But there were also the glaucous and waxy grey-whites, a refinement which I urge on all white gardeners.

Whoever suggested the slate-white hanging tube-flowers of a campanula called *burghaltii* deserves my prize for ingenious planting. In full flower, this abundant plant took the edge off the bright whiteness of the main theme, for white is itself a very strong colour. This grey-white campanula was well mixed with the glaucous leaves and flowers of hostas, and the grey-white spots on the leaves of the ordinary spring-flowering Spotted Dog, a plant untidy elsewhere but improved beyond recognition by its surrounding of bright white flower and dark green yew hedge.

Like grey, a greenish-yellow and dark evergreen leaf bring the best out of white which is concentrated in small, bold groups: I suspect I am right in accusing the National Trust of introducing too many white Iceberg roses into an originally off-white design, as Iceberg was barely in commerce when Vita Sackville-West died. It is an interesting warning that in a white garden, two-thirds of this white rose would be better removed for being too blatant. I would rather see white valerian, our plainer native flower.

But there could be no hope of moving the garden's glory, surely planted in the first design, a thriving clump of the 7-foot-high lily-like cardiocrinum, whose glossy and fleshy round leaves and enormous downturned trumpets of sweet white flowers summed up the whole strength of the garden's whiteness. There is no more spectacular plant, but I have never made it grow, perhaps because I own no shaded woodland. This giant lily is happiest in leafy soil.

The success of this white garden, in fact, is that it is not really white. By all means imitate it, but the one idea of whiteness, blueness or pinkness only makes a collection, not a garden. You may feel, as I do, that it is timid to copy others' ideas; you may well wonder whether a garden based on black-purple against a grey-leaved hedge might not be a novel alternative. But if you go white by night and enjoy your own Sissinghurst on a summer evening, having copied the whole idea at home, I cannot blame you for wanting something so lovely. But there is only one home for each idea, and I doubt if you will ever balance out the result so beautifully again.

Whenever a lady first comes into possession of a country garden, she begins to think she wants a patch of herbs. Near the kitchen, she thinks, so that she can hurry out and pick bunches of fennel for her boiled turbot; plenty of variety, she hopes, as books are always talking about hyssop for the honey, tansy for head-colds, rue for brown bread sandwiches, and lashings of penny-royal, which is said to cure depressions. So, next Christmas, husband

Above: *Pyrus salicifolia pendula,* Weeping Silver Pear at Sissinghurst. Up to 15 ft, but is almost prettier in most gardens in an upright form, 20–25 ft. No pruning, negligible flowers. Becoming a status symbol

Below: The White Garden at Sissinghurst

gives her a novelty pack of herb seeds, clears a patch near the kitchen and leaves her to learn that weeds are very determined, winters cold and recipes often misleading.

Herbal lore and country remedies are two fields of knowledge which, mostly, I have no wish whatsoever to try to master. I would rather buy my jam and have time to read a book than spend three days in making it from home-grown fruit. Cans save the bother of bottling; peppermint tea seems considerably less effective for my headaches than a dose of aspirin. Count me out, if it is old wives' cunning you are wanting, as one of the twentieth-century's achievements is to have decided to kill it off. Morris dancing still lingers but, by and large, we are taking the olde-tyme merriness out of the English countryside. About time too, and as a gardener, not a cook, I feel the same about most herb gardens.

Herb gardens have a way of intruding into designs by default. You have placed the roses, the herbaceous, the lavender edging and the blossoming cherries, and you are left with an awkward rectangle behind your newly planted hedge, preferably not of that brilliant green conifer if you value this book at all. Somebody mentions herbs as the right sort of romantic addition to a country garden, so you seize on the remaining rectangle and begin to plan camomile paths, small thyme lawns and a clump of heart's-ease to keep out visiting witches. Dressed in a frilly sunhat, madam will be able to trip daintily down to cull basil and strew it in her trug, while fumitory protects her from pixies, the breath of tarragon deals with her neckaches and valerian gives her cat the time of its life. A small adjustment of the bodice, and we might be back in the fifteenth century.

No, most emphatically, a herbery is not for me. Obedient to Boulestin's recipes, I have taken rue sandwiches and tried to pretend they were helping my eyesight. I have picked the candied angelica off party cakes and wished, from the earliest age, that this bold green-flowered garden plant was kept out of the *pâtisserie* where it does not belong. Dandelion wine is a perversity; less so, nettle soup, but I would never choose to pick the ingredients. For gardeners herbs mean hard work, frequent renewal and, usually, a patch of unkempt ugliness.

As a general garden rule, I do not like segregation. I like to see vegetables among flowers in the front garden, and I would only consider a rose garden if I was allowed to underplant it, a habit, incidentally, which does not harm the rose bushes as long as they are heavily fed with liquid manure. Herbs, mostly, are rank-growing and floppy, never at their neatest when flowering or flowered. In an exclusively herbal corner, they often look boring rather than romantic. I prefer to break them up and put them to their different aesthetic uses.

Take tarragon, for instance; this seems to me to be a culinary necessity, if only for any roast chicken or tartar sauce, and yet it is lanky and extremely dull to grow. It insists on well-drained warm soil, and together with basil, another undistinguished plant,

Above: The Herb Garden, Sissinghurst: one of a few exceptions to my view on unkempt herb-patches

Below: Thyme lawn of *drucei,* Pink Chintz, *albus:* pretty, but needs maintenance until established. Extremely easy to increase by cuttings or runners from one parent, each set 9 in or so apart. Not always weed-proof

Right: *Mentha gracilis,* prettier and neater form of mint. Spreads, especially in cool semi-shade. Up to one foot

Left: *Foeniculum vulgare,* Fennel, herb for fish and for caterpillars of the Swallow Tail butterfly. Flowers June–July; 4 ft. Any soil, likes lime and sun. Very free seeding

it is as difficult to please as any herb. But it barely competes with tansy, one of the bitterest and least sympathetic plants I can think of as I write, or with wormwood, so much uglier than other artemisias and useless unless you are being crucified, or with woad, which may have dyed our forefathers blue but is quite incapable of turning us green with envy. Yet herb gardens often have all four together.

And yet, of course, I do not hate all herbs. It is just that few find their way palatably into cooking, and it is sheer sentimentality to pretend that the rest are of such garden value that they deserve a corner entirely to themselves.

I would never wish to be without fennel, so decorative in youth, middle age, yellow-green flower and spilling seed. Rosemary is a necessity, for looks as much as for roast chicken (you must be thinking I eat nothing else); the finest mint is the white variegated form, which can hold its own in any shady border, besides adding flavour to the new potatoes.

Hyssop is a charming autumn shrub, but herbally futile unless you keep bees. I am not hostile to herbs but rather to the useless recommendations which herbalists try to foist on to us gardeners. I quote, for instance, the virtues of cumin, one of the washiest purple weeds I have ever seen. It 'occurs in the Bible, heals the eyes; adds pallor to the cheeks and prevents fickleness in love'. Give me a godless red-faced Casanova and a garden free of such clutter. You can stop your cumin, as far as my garden is concerned, for these are not the virtues for which I would give space to a plant, let alone to a new design.

'When all is said and done, is there any more wonderful sight, any moment when man's reason is nearer to some sort of contact with the nature of the world than the sowing of seeds, the planting of cuttings, the transplanting of shrubs or the grafting of slips? It is as if you could question the vital force in each root or bud on what it can do, what it cannot and why.'

So thought St Augustine in one of his less intransigent moments as a local African bishop: in his later years, it did not occur to him that faith too can be propagated as gently and peaceably as an oleander. But even some 1500 years later, keen gardeners still share that contact with the nature of the world which he had the insight to appreciate; gardening is seldom more satisfactory than when it raises new children from old.

The two weeks in mid-July are the moment to be busy. Cuttings, especially, must be well-timed as even those plants which will root at any time of year grow faster at some seasons than at others: July is my moment for boxfuls of audacious cuttings. Some die, others are neglected, and others root too readily for me to use them all, but even when my garden seems finally to be full I will indulge in yearly propagation just for the sake of wonder that despite my fingers the process still works.

Of all the methods, cuttings amaze me most, possibly because cuttings come directly from one chosen and long-loved plant. Though they have their peculiarities, some will root even if these are ignored; there is, however, a routine which I have long used and therefore like to think has been responsible for my successes. Like Adam and Eve, I have no mist propagator.

My cuttings go into pots and boxes, thickly spaced but never so close that their leaves touch. Their earth is mixed to an unforgettable recipe which is called one, two, three; one part by bulk of sieved garden soil, two parts of peat and three parts of coarse sand. Builders' sand is useless and poor quality peat is a waste of money. I mix this up, having made sure that it has been watered and allowed to settle down to being moist, not boggy.

Armed with a razor blade, or, failing that, a kitchen knife, I then take the filled pot over to the plant. I choose a plant which is young and healthy as cuttings from the aged are more troublesome; at this time of the year, it will probably be a shrub.

Assume for the sake of an example that it is an orange blossom, now 50p a time from a nursery but absurdly easy for an amateur to root free of charge for himself. It has just finished flowering and then is the moment to strike. It is thick with next year's flowering shoots, young, not too sappy and springing from a hard branch. I take one young shoot near where it joins old wood and pull it gently away with my fingers, trying to bring a 'heel' of old wood off with it; the heel must be short and thin.

Pessimistically, I take twice as many as I need. As each is taken, I slip it into the propagator's secret weapon: the polythene bag. Once inside, it will not wilt dramatically; if it does, seal the bag with a few drops of water inside it and wait till the cuttings recover. This tip for taking cuttings is one among many to be learnt from Christopher Lloyd's excellent *Well-Tempered Garden*.

One by one, I take them from the bag and trim them with the razor blade. For at least one-third of their length I slice off their leaves, being most careful not to graze the main skin. If necessary I cut off their tops, believing that 6 inches is as much length as a usual cutting needs. Straight from the knife, I plant each one very firmly near the side of its pot, where drainage is better, and thus give it no time to sweat and flag. I push the earth hard round it so that it will not come out when lightly pulled. I test it by pulling it once to make sure.

Four cuttings to a 5-inch pot are quite enough; one-third of their length should be under the earth, so that no leaves are buried or in contact with the surface of the soil. Once the little hopefuls are in, I take the pot back to the house and busy myself with twigs and sticks. This is the point where I usually lose my temper twice before succeeding; the aim is to use the sort of twigs which stake other people's winter hyacinths and push them down into the pot's earth at all angles, vertically, near-horizontally and, if there is room, in between, in order to make a framework over which to slip the polythene bag. Wire, if you have it, might well be easier.

The whole point is to stop the bag from touching the cuttings at any point. If it does, the drops of water which sweat on to it will help the leaves to rot and rotting cuttings are not likely to survive. The sticks need to be broken and placed carefully so as not to dislodge the cuttings; the polythene bag has to be the right width and as mine either began life holding jerseys or spare parts for the noisy Hoover, this is seldom the case. Hence the bad temper, but once the bag is properly over the sticks and the pot, head first, its neck is easily fixed tight with a rubber band round the pot's lower reaches. The whole outfit is then best stood in semi-shade or on a west-facing window sill; a cold frame is ideal, a greenhouse suitable but unnecessary. The bag is to be kept closed. This is most important.

The cuttings must not dry out but, thanks to the polythene and the sand, frequent watering will not be needed. Inspect them every five days or so and as soon as you see signs that your cuttings are growing, not marking time, then slit the polythene bag above their heads. Give them another few days to get used to fresh air and then take the bag off altogether: if the cuttings keep on growing as they should, transplant them very soon to a small pot of their own. But remember to take them forwards by stages once you see signs of success. It is a severe shock to come out of a polythene bag which has been over one's head for a fortnight.

On no account pull the cuttings out of the earth in order to see how they are getting on; curiosity is forgivable but if you must inspect them before they show signs of growth, tap the ball of earth out of the pot and see if there are signs of roots down its side. If the cuttings are firmly planted and settled in damp earth, they probably will not fall out in the meantime. But it is better to

leave them well alone, time notwithstanding. I once rooted an osmanthus after fifteen months.

So much, then, for the broad procedure; next I will fill in a few details and suggest those shrubs which are most likely to succeed. Even St Augustine would not have been so enthusiastic if his monks had tried to root the common but obstinate lilac. Wonderment is very much the privilege of the successful.

It is here that enthusiasm gets the better of ability; not just one of my neighbour's pink ceanothus, I tell myself, as it dangles enticingly against her wall; why not take ten or twenty and hedge my bets against the killing frosts it so detests? A forest of philadelphus, a grove of gingko and all among them honeysuckles of every kind; where parents are waiting for the propagator, it is easy to think in lavish terms.

Three months later sense returns, as every rooted cutting needs repotting and there is never room for them all. Those who like cuttings always have too many plants. But there are few better presents to give away.

Sometimes, this multiplying is ludicrously easy. Last March I sowed many different kinds of violet seed in an old kipper box and as I had to keep each variety in its own compartment, I partitioned them off with thick twigs of yellow dogwood, cut haphazardly and shorn of its leaves. None of the violets has come up but in their place I now have four new plants of dogwood, rooted all along the twigs which were lying flat and neglected for the past four months. In April, I cut a few branches of the red flowering currant and put them in a vase of water: when I threw them out belatedly, they had already begun to root in the water.

There is a lesson, I now read, to be learnt from these accidents. Each October, near-hardy shrubs like fuchsias or hebes are combed for cuttings by gardeners who are too wise to risk losing them to a sharp frost. These cuttings too can be sunk for half their length in a jar of water, just like my ribes, and allowed to make underwater roots: the water soon turns green, but it is no hardship to change it regularly and keep it sweet by putting a piece of charcoal at the bottom. The jar can be stood on a light window sill where roots can be kept under observation: I am enjoying six lilac-pink penstemons at the moment which rooted in a kitchen glass during last year's electricity cuts.

Polythene and pots of sand are often just as easy. The sandy earth does not need watering, the polythene (if well-stretched so as not to touch the cuttings) does not need wiping and there are any number of willing shrubs waiting to be tried. At first avoid lilacs and viburnums, camellias, and most mahonias, as they are either very slow or very difficult; the perfect beginners' cuttings are sun roses *(Helianthemum),* orange blossom *(Philadelphus),* honey-suckles, cotton lavender, thymes and most of the grey-leaved plants which lift any garden out of a rut. Buddleia, Japanese quince, honeysuckles, *Rubus tridel,* caryopteris, ceratostigma and senecio are equally easy. So, too, are the popular shrub poten-

Penstemon George Home. Flowers July–September. 2 ft high. Do not cut down in autumn; best in warm sunny corner, though fairly hardy anywhere. Cuttings are easy, and autumn ones can be wintered under glass as a precaution. Likes lime, worth dead-heading

tillas once you learn that surprising readiness to root in late Autumn from shoots which are just shedding flower.

All of these can best be taken now, from healthy wood which, for preference, has not flowered; none needs a greenhouse or cold frame. If you want to save labour and go in for ground cover, smothering one weed with another, cuttings are one way to cover a large area without spending an equally large sum of money.

Adventure, however, can bring more surprising rewards, especially from shrubs with firm fleshy stems. If you see a flourishing bush of the mexican orange *(Choisya ternata)* in the next few weeks, be sure to ask permission to cut a few young shoots beneath a nobbly joint and slip them into your pocket; three of these set in a 5-inch pot should be well away by the beginning of September. The glorious *Daphne odora* in its golden leaved form is so sweet-scented in flower in early spring that it is almost worth paying the nurserymen's high prices for half a dozen. But again, under my polythene bag, short cuttings taken beneath a hard joint in mid-July will show every sign of rooting happily. I take as many as possible, to set them under every available house window and enjoy their smell; they are not, however, for sunless walls or northern counties. The many sickly-smelling skimmias are other winter evergreens which are expensive to buy and astonishingly easy to root at home. Six of these are never too many for a shady drive or north-facing backyard.

Every summer I am swept along by thoughts of edging the entire garden with pinks. I was given one laced variety two years ago and I have so far turned it into another sixty-two, waiting for their show of chocolate-and-white patterned flowers next June and July. They are not the easiest of cuttings, partly because it is so easy to cut them wrong. I often find I have taken a shoot with a

Right: *Skimmia japonica*, female form with red winter berries. Happy in shade, prefers no lime. Up to 5 ft. Very easy indeed from cuttings

hollow tube of stalk at the end instead of a lumpy joint. It is tempting to pinch out the cuttings with your fingers but a razor blade gives much neater, firmer results. I hope for two hundred successes in the following four weeks, a saving of some £50.

How confident this sounds and how close to becoming too sure of the job; one night I walked in through the shadows, pinks in polythene behind me, and suddenly caught the scent of the year's first flower on *Magnolia grandiflora*, lemon-scented, spice-laden, as cold as an empty church. Its crumpled white petals defied me to try my luck with them. The razor blade advanced, steadied, then withdrew; ten years had passed till that magnolia had flowered, and it did not seem right to meddle with its long glossy leaves. Even to the propagator, certain shrubs remain private. *Magnolia grandiflora,* though willing in principle to root, made my polythene bags seem very humble affairs.

After a recent visit to Italy, I find much that I would like to do in my garden. This can be dangerous, as Mediterranean ideas do not transplant very easily to England. Vines on poles and pergolas never quite feel the same in a sodden English summer, while olive trees and oranges in ornamental pots will not survive our usual winters.

I have seen the true pencil-shaped cypresses, such as feature in the background of the Italian Renaissance pictures, not the glaucous and feathery kinds in a garden centre, growing well against a wall in Warwickshire, but I would be reluctant to risk them in an exposed position myself. Nevertheless, another country's gardening always starts up a few ideas that the climate cannot damage.

In Rome, it is hard to escape the acanthus for long. I have often wondered why we do not make more intelligent use of it here. Climate is not really the reason, for though an acanthus's leaves last through the winter in southern Italy and spread on to any patch of open ground, the best kinds are nearly evergreen in milder English gardens too. Here, they are quite willing to stretch themselves among their neighbours.

In Italy, the acanthus seldom has flowery neighbours, as the flower-border is not an Italian feature. It looks even better for their absence. If you have never met an acanthus but have looked at architecture, Greek if possible, you will know what it looks like, as it has been carved on pillars for two thousand years. Long, glossy green leaves, prickly and rather similar to those of a globe artichoke, reach a height of about two feet and then throw up straight spikes of hooded vanilla and white flowers in August, equipped with a thorny hook which has earned them the unattractive name of Bear's Breeches.

You will like them as long as you do not handle them, but it is the leaves, I hope, which will most catch your fancy. Usually, they are concealed in a late-summer flower border and placed for their flowers only. Their outline is lost in a mass of phlox and daisies and visitors wonder why anybody bothered to plant them.

But the place for an acanthus should be special, a bed of its

Acanthus spinosus. August flowering; 3–4 ft. Prickly leaves. Slow at first, then runs widely. Runners can be detached quite simply

own where it can be viewed from all sides, or a place of emphasis, at the bottom of a statue or on the corner of a path or at the foot of a wall, where its flowers can be cut off if they look too tall for the glossy green of the leaf In Italy, it appears at the foot of old box hedges, beside an ornamental flower-pot or even in the formal paving of a country villa's terrace. It is one more evergreen brick from which gardens are built.

Which kind, then, to choose? Experiment convinces me that care is needed. The freest flowering is a kind called *longifolius,* but its leaves are not so magnificent. As I am interested in the leaves, I would urge you to two more usual varieties. Of these, *mollis* is the best known, as its leaves are large and as soft to the touch as their Latin name implies. At least near London, they will sometimes last right through the winter until a very sharp frost or heavy fall of snow. They are not, however, my favourite.

Here, the honours go to a slightly smaller-leaved one called *spinosus,* which is as firm and prickly as its name. It glistens more healthily than *mollis* and has a more clearly-defined look to it, which is exactly right for an isolated planting. The superlative form *spinosissimus* turns up occasionally but is no improvement, having leaves of a less good green and a more prickly shape. Alpine nurseries sometimes offer one called *carolus-alexandri,* which is about two feet tall, but after six years of effort, I have still to make it flower.

So at ground level you have your well-placed acanthus, preferably *spinosus,* and above it, swayed by Italy, I would be tempted to try a Judas tree. You see this at its finest in Venice, surrounded by festoons of wistaria and reflected in the grey-green of the canals. In our own home counties, it can look remarkably effective in the May following a hot summer.

A good lilac year is also a good Judas year. Its leaves are small and heart-shaped and its flowers are a bright rosy pink, nearer the rose than the pink, but nonetheless delightful. For a normal lifespan, it is a splendid small garden tree, though I have seen one at Kew which must be over thirty feet tall. Its flowers can even be eaten in salads, a popular dish in Greece and always to be risked as it is free from the curse of their cooking oil.

But there is one drawback to a Judas; your garden must be warm and sunny if it is ever to flower properly. It is a myth that Judas ever hanged himself on its branches, as they were far too brittle, and one historian, at least, thought Judas tripped and burst apart, with his feet on the ground. It is true, however, that this tree will betray you unless you are patient with it and give it a sunny home. Then you can train it, as in Italy, into a tunnel on hoops and wires, but you must be prepared to wait for it to become established. And I cannot promise it will flower.

The same patience suits acanthus, which will creep along very slowly for three or four years and then suddenly outpace all else in the garden. If you give in to a European idea, it is no use becoming impatient rooting out a young acanthus, or chopping

Cercis siliquastrum, Judas Tree. Up to 20 ft. Flowers May–June. Needs sun and warmth if it is to flower at all. Pretty leaf, and pretty when trained as a tunnel or on a pergola. Otherwise no pruning. Will grow from seed, but too slowly

down a shy-flowering Judas. The results will come, but they take several seasons and only then do they make the years of waiting seem worthwhile.

A sudden string of inquiries about climbing roses has made me look back and discover that I have never really noted down what I feel about them. I love them, of course, but it is only worth choosing the best, and I am never quite sure which I consider to be the best from one year to the next. My current opinions are as follows.

If you have plenty of room and want something to grow quickly I do not think you can do much better than the warm pink rambler Albertine. I would say that I have never known this fail had I not planted one recently on a corner of my mother-in-law's house where it is shaded by a high yew hedge and scoured by a north-west wind which comes through the gap of a nearby garden gate. After two years it looks very scrawny, and this only goes to prove that no worthwhile plant is tough enough to grow anywhere. Against an ordinary north or east wall, Albertine will ramble fast and thick. It is quite a business to keep wiring back the new growths which it makes with great rapidity from May until autumn.

Albertine throws out long new shoots and tends to flower in the middle of its tangle where the older growth of the previous year has been left behind. It is sensible to prune it hard in July after flowering so that all its next season's flower shoots start off at the same level. Its growth, too, is so vigorous that a mid-season trimming is often a relief. Do not be afraid to attack it at this unusual time of the year. You can stick some of the shoots you have cut off into a sandy trench out of direct sunlight and you will find they root most obligingly, especially if you bury half their length in the earth. Not many gardens can house more than two Albertines, so you will have to give them away as prickly Christmas presents. Its thorns are very unpleasant.

No rose is ever perfect and Albertine, I grant you, only flowers once, though profusely. Do not expect flowers of a classically pointed shape, for the promising buds of a dark rose pink open to a floppy and somewhat fluffy flower which has been compared to a pink rose dipped in a cup of tea. I am not sure that it is entirely apt, though there is a warm suffusion through Albertine's petals.

It does not smell of stale teacups, however, so those of you who hate that particular flavour of drowsy office corridors in late afternoon need not be deterred. Equally, it does not smell much of roses either. But a kind word should be said for its shining leaves, rose-copper when young, even though they do catch mildew quite often. Ignore mildew on an Albertine. It soon shakes it off in a mass of new growth. It only flowers once, in late June, so the late summer peak of mildew does not affect its performance.

Still on the fast and tough growers, I recommend you to Albertine's neighbour in catalogues called Alberic Barbier. White-flowered with a yellowish tinge, remarkably rapid, apt to keep its leaves for most of the winter, this rose has given me the greatest pleasure over an iron pergola even though it only flowers once and has no more shape or scent than Albertine. A north wall does not defeat it. After fourteen years, our finest specimen is dying back on shoots that have flowered, and I wish I knew why. Perhaps a hard cutting will revive its vigour. Elsewhere it lives to such an age that its base can become like a small tree trunk.

Leaving aside even faster growers, including a favourite of mine called Rambling Rector, which makes very much quicker headway than any of the church dignitaries after which it is named, I come to the climber which I would take to a well-mulched desert island in preference to any other.

It is that old favourite called New Dawn. Every year I marvel at its colour, a pale pink-white which ages to an even purer sort of ghostly blush. This admirable rose only comes into its own in mid-July on our north wall; there it shows behind an August border whose tall back-row plants are not then up to their full height. If it catches a disease it always shakes it off; its leaves, a feature of a rose which deserves more attention, are a dark, glossy green, and its crop of flower is always heavy.

Please do not be deceived by a variation called Red New Dawn or Etendard. This is the crudest sort of carmine and seems to blink at you on bright days. I rate it with the violent Danse du Feu for effrontery; their colours are too often seen against new brick walls where they clash as well as clamour. Always consult your climbing rose's background. I know nothing prettier than a clear, but not too buttery, yellow against grey stone or concrete, first choice here being the old but admirable Lawrence Johnston. Golden Showers would last longer in flower, but it also has a metallic look about it which is not balanced out by its commendable resistance to wet weather. The background to a climber is so important and Golden Showers does not always fit it. The coppery pink shrub rose Aloha can also be trained up a wall for a long-lasting effect, and it is not deterred by heavy rain.

Owners of mellowed houses will have to look far to beat the old Gloire de Dijon, an extremely long-flowering rose whose quartered and flattish flowers of buff-apricot are born freely, but not so freely that they cannot be sniffed and admired individually. North or east walls will suffice for it, but it does become leggy with age, however carefully you prune and train it. It is also a devil for disease, especially black spot.

It has been around for many years and when I look back at Edwardian photographs of vigorous specimens reaching to the eaves and stretching right to the ground I often wonder whether it has lost its impetus over the years. It is an old friend and a familiar one, but as with Albertine and the beautiful New Dawn, familiarity is no failing in the choosing of a climbing rose.

The most difficult of a gardener's choices is that of a tree. This came home to me while reading a letter from a gardener who complained about his crop of conkers. How, he wished to know, could

Koelreuteria paniculata, Golden Rain Tree. Up to 20 ft; spreading. Flowers July–August, best in hot summers. Autumn colour and fruits

he stop his horse chestnut from producing conkers so that gangs of boys would not pelt his tree with sticks and disfigure it and the surrounding garden? I lived with the same menace from an old and abundant walnut until we warned the attackers that if they pelted the tree once more for its fruit we would send for a policeman; they stopped, but so did the tree, for it has not cropped properly since. Threats, it would seem, are not a prudent answer.

There is, of course, no way to stop a flowering tree from fruiting, unless you choose to pick off all its flower buds. Nobody would wish to dead-head a massive horse chestnut, so the only advice is the useless advice to choose a safer horse chestnut in the first place. It is not well enough known that certain hybrids in the *Aesculus* group, the horse chestnut's home in a catalogue, will flower but not follow flowers with conkers, being sterile and fruitless.

A variation on the familiar *carnea,* called *plantierensis,* bears narrower leaves than the usual fishbone style and carries pink flowers on its rounded shape without producing any fruits. These *carnea* chestnut trees are the smaller rose-pink varieties which used to be planted round cricket grounds and leave room for batsmen to hit a six over their tops. They are a hybrid, surprisingly, between an American chestnut called a buck-eye and the true chestnut which is so admired by visitors to Turkey and the Balkans. It would need more than Sobers to hit a ball over this gigantic tree whose older specimens exceed 100 feet and whose fawn-white flowers stand out like candles from top to bottom.

Please do not plant this giant in your back garden or too near your house. If you must have a chestnut there, try a form of *carnea* but remember how the dense leaves of these trees suck several hundred gallons of water a day out of the earth around them. A horse chestnut is not at ease in a dry summer nor on hot quick-draining soil, most often to be found in alkaline areas. It is not a tree under which you can plant shade-loving flowers.

So my choice of chestnut for a small garden would have to be less familiar in order to suit its space. There is a cousin of the chestnuts called *Koelreuteria paniculata* which is a sensible choice for small spaces because it has virtues which prolong its season.

I have never seen it more than twenty-five feet tall and I would always plant it in a sunny place in soil which was not too rich; a summer as dry as our recent one suits it very well. It is a tree with a bold and interesting leaf, pinnate, as botanists call it, or feathery as I describe it, in the way that an enlarged acacia leaf or a shortened Tree of Heaven leaf would be feathery and elegant. When these leaves appear in spring they are a reddish brown for a week or two before taking on a normal green. Flowers appear in dry summers during late July and August; they are pretty, discreet and, to my eye, thoroughly charming.

A popular name for this tree, which few gardeners plant, is the Golden Rain tree because the strings of small yellow flowers,

Top left: *Rubus × tridel.* 7 ft × 7 ft, May flowering. Any soil especially lime, chalk and sun. Lovely in informal hedges. Quick-growing, and most easy from cuttings taken in June–July. No pruning, unless necessary for space. A favourite of mine

Top right: *Buddleia alternifolia,* up to 15 ft on wall or as a loose standard tree, when trained. Likes some sun, very easy. Can be trimmed in July after flowering. Will root from long cuttings then

Bottom left: *Mesembryanthemum criniflorum,* Livingstone Daisy. Half-hardy annual, 3 in high. Sow under glass in early May, not earlier as it damps off too easily. Space out c. 1 ft apart in June. Needs sun and drought; good on walls, paths, paving. Dead-head

Bottom right: *Gazania leucoleana.* Half-hardy annual. Flowers July–September. c. 18 in high. Sow under glass in March; plant in very sunny site in June. Not obliging. Best colours should be retained in autumn cuttings

red-centred and strung on their stems like a bracelet, are left to hang down from the leaves like the inverted flower of a horse chestnut. A dry autumn gives you bronze seedpods shaped like a bladder, as in some of those late summer shrubs which are cousins to the pea family; these are worth studying, but the Golden Rain tree's autumn colour is far more noticeable.

It grows into a pleasantly open shape and spreads these yellow autumn leaves to their advantage; I had always assumed its natural home was China, for it had that unusual grace which is commonly ascribed to inaccessible Chinese plants. So indeed it proves, as I look it up in its catalogue; the gardener who will be prouder of a 20-foot-high Golden Rain tree after twenty years than of a 20-foot-high poplar after ten should take this *Koelreuteria* to heart. It is a sensible choice, and the man who plants trees, of all things, has to choose sensibly, for he cannot waste time on mistakes.

'Marigolds obey the sun,' wrote King Charles I towards the end of his stay in prison, 'More than my subjects me have done.' A vintage year for marigolds is also a vintage year for claret, fig trees and batsmen, all of whom obey long hours of sunshine. Sunshine makes a marigold gleam, in science as well as its owner's imagination. On clear evenings after a sunny spell, even the critical eye of Charles Darwin noticed that marigolds seem to give off a bright flash of light from their petals.

I have never looked for this as I rate the marigold, except the single-pot marigold, very low among annuals. I do not like its stiffness and dank leaf and the stench of stale tea leaves which comes from its stems and flowers in wet weather. I would not believe its flash of light if Darwin had not observed it: I wonder whether gardeners who grow marigolds, the most popular annual in England, have memories of evenings after work, lit by a flash from their marigold's flowerbed.

My own feeling, when marigolds are flashing most brightly, is that this is a season in which I should be growing annuals from South Africa. When the marigolds signal fine weather, the brilliant daisies from the veldt and lower hill-slopes are set fair for the summer. Their names deter the unadventurous who will not succeed with them anyway: *Gazania, Dimorphotheca* (a botanical word to mean a flower with two shapes of seed-vessel), *Ursinia, Arctotis, Mesembryanthemum* (or Livingstone Daisy) and *Venidium*. I list them in descending order of excellence.

All these long names have flowers like a large and exotic daisy and are half-hardy, needing to be sown in a greenhouse in early April and to be pricked out three weeks later and planted outside in early June. Devoted dead-heading will keep them flowering from late June to October and while away the slow, spare hours of a Sunday evening, to great effect if you are careful to remove every single one of their faded flowers. In dull weather they close their petals tightly, like an umbrella held upright. These petals are attached to a dark daisy-disc in their centre which contrasts

Above: *Dimorphotheca*. Flowers July–September, easy annual. Can be sown directly outdoors in mid-May; best sown under glass in April. Space out in June. Dead-head, and save next year's seed in early October

Below: *Dimorphotheca ecklonis*. Another variety requiring similar treatment and conditions. White-flowered with indigo centre. Likes sun and drought. Beautiful on walls or slopes. Increase by cuttings in autumn, wintered indoors

prettily with their orange and ivory colouring.

Ursinia is the least varied, being a clear silky orange with a chestnut-brown ring at its base. It grows 9 inches high, flowers unforgettably freely and would make an unusual edging in place of those mats of white alyssum.

The Livingstone Daisy is lower, more familiar and many-coloured. Its fleshy leaves of grey-green are marked with small crystals, like grains of sugar, and hold the drops of water which they need in their arid home ground. This fleshiness should persuade you to plant them on top of dry walls or at the edge of gravel paths where there is sharp drainage and little water. They spread into a mat about a foot wide and flower very brightly. It is a grave mistake to sow their seed too soon in a greenhouse or warm room. A mid-April sowing times their season sensibly, or even an early May one. Do not be talked into starting them in March, for they will damp off as seedlings or suffer a check when they have rooted and grown on too early. They never fully recover.

Of venidium I say less except to remind you that it is 2 feet tall and a gay orange with a brown stripe again: venidiums have been crossed with arctotis to give a plant with an even longer name which has the advantage of arctotis's shades of pink and ivory white. Suttons Seeds of Reading are the specialists and moving spirits here, but I would still prefer the smaller-flowered and more dependable dimorphotheca.

This is a name that ought to be far more widely known, especially in the pure white form called *ecklonis* which begins with a blue-black base to its petals, then fades to a snow-white all over. Seed is now available from Thompson and Morgan, sellers of these other South Africans, at London Road, Ipswich. This plant can be massed on a bank for its autumn flowers which are born on carpets of leaves. It is not hardy, but cuttings are easily rooted in October and wintered in a room or cellar. The shades of colour in this plant's many annual forms are a lasting wonder. Apricot, yellow, ivory, coral and rose-pink combine in a range which only dignifies South African daisies. They are very easy to grow and reach a height of 18 inches at most.

For colouring and style, however, the prize goes to the infamous gazania. I say infamous, because this plant is dependent on fine weather and careful gardening. Its tones of colour include a pink-grey, a pink-orange which wallpaper makers call sunset and a selection of tangerines, buff-yellows and raspberry pinks which I do not think you will find in any other plant. A green-grey leaf displays them to their full advantage.

But gazanias are not easily sustained from seed nor humoured in wet weather; the cure, I am certain, is to take cuttings of all colours after a superb season and winter them in a cold room or frame, avoiding seed altogether. You have to get started, though, and there is a case for buying gazanias direct from the shops as small plants in June (not May) and planting them beneath a south wall or as the edging to a sunny path.

September

The more we become accustomed to clear and sunny autumn weather, the more the months of September and October should be designed as a delight in the garden's year, a test of ingenuity. There is an acrid smell about autumn's Michaelmas daisies and bronze-yellow heleniums which I always notice on the green canvas of the flower shows' stands. They do not come high in my favour for autumn: there is no pleasure in a Michaelmas daisy for most of the year, and lovely though a lavender-blue hybrid called *Aster frikartii* would look in place of many more familiarly-named varieties, the smell and the short season of the ordinary Michaelmas daisies' flowers would usually turn me away from them.

I am much more attracted by fruits, not the apples which are always crisper, to put it politely, than I expect or the pears whose skins are as thick as those of any public figure, but the fruits of roses, shrubs, mountain ashes and decorative onions. Here, it is worth exploring and experimenting, a gardener's keenest pleasure.

The autumn onions to which I refer are the paper-brown seedheads of the ornamental bulbs called alliums. The flowers, mostly, are rose-purple or lilac-purple, though there are some kingfisher blues which are needlessly unpopular; in autumn these flowers have disappeared, and careful gardeners are left with a dried brown seedhead like a major's drumstick, in which the black onion-seeds glisten and rustle, ready for collection.

The seedheads can be cut and used in vases for winter decoration, along with autumn's teasels and pampas grasses: the most effective ones are borne by a 4-foot-high allium called *schubertii*, after the composer, I like to imagine, and very harmonious in rose-lilac flower and dried brown old age. It is becoming very fashionable, for the branches in its seedheads are as clearly defined as the struts or girders in an architect's designs. A valuable autumn contrast can be enjoyed from this ornamental onion, and is matched by two others called *albo-pilosum,* more magnificent in full flower in June, and *afflatunense*, slenderer and slightly cheaper. Their flowers do smell of onion but I cannot think why you should wish to sniff them. The dried heads are quite unscented.

If a dead-head seems depressing, it can be cheered up by the gay colour and enticing shape of rose-hips. One of the many disadvantages of growing modern floribundas is their lack of this sensational second season; they do not fruit brightly, whereas the shrub rose called *moyesii* in its several forms enlivens September with masses of scarlet hips, as prominent as any autumn crop of rose buds. This is a vigorous shrub rose for tough grass, orchards or the edges of lightly shaded woods where it will arch prettily into a wide and tall specimen. I have neither wood nor orchard so I have never planted it, not least because its single flowers seem to me to be over-rated, even in the matt scarlet form called geranium. But its hips are magnificent and I can only console myself with the bright, more delicately shaped fruits of the very different *Rosa rubrifolia*.

This rose mixes impressively in any border of flowers where its grey-purple leaves stand out as an individual grouping. I can imagine an unusual planting of a glossy evergreen – the smooth leaved holly called *Ilex camelliaefolia* would be excellent – broken up by clumps of *Rosa rubrifolia* for 6-foot-high branches of delicate leaf and fruit. I remember a gardener who wrote to tell me of a border planted with a drift of this rose and a group of the variegated dogwood. It sounded very sophisticated then and I am sure it would look pretty if tried now.

Red fruits and berries, of course, are autumn's familiar attraction; how many gardeners, though, take the yellow-green fruits of their spring-flowering quinces (or japonicas) seriously? I have resolved to pay more attention to this second effect of a shrub which has few equals for massed wild planting or decorative woodland thickets. We should all plant, too, for the scarlet berries of viburnums, especially the enormously heavy trusses of a kind called *betulifolium* and the bright bunches of a form of the Guelder rose *(Viburnum opulus)* sold as Notcutt's variety.

The pink marbles borne as fruits by forms of the mountain ash, such as *Sorbus vilmorinii,* should not be ignored, either, by any garden in need of a small tree with many seasonal virtues. But pleasures such as the knobbled and inedible fruits of a flowering quince are often overlooked and ignored, an added blessing which we do not take into account. No gardener can afford to make too little of his plants, least of all in autumn when the sun is having its

Above: *Allium triquetrum.* Lovely, vigorous Wild Onion. Up to 12 in, bulb. April flowering. Happy in shade or wild gardens. Spreads freely when suited. Worth growing more often

Right: *Ilex aquifolium argenteo-marginata elegantissima.* A male holly, prickly. No berries

last and longest run. We must be attentive, for what we miss in autumn will not be there as a memory to help us through the winter.

September is the month when the garden can do with some convolvulus. This may sound like madness but it has already struck me twice in the past week and I intend to follow up the idea. The hedgerows and the roadsides should be inspected in case you are incredulous. There are patches of browned nettles, one of the distinguishing uglinesses of Britain's common flora; there is thistle down, a wonderful thing, certainly, but only born on plants that are near senility. The one fresh feature is the bindweed in its two main forms. In Sussex they used to refer to the white trumpet-flowered bindweeds as 'lilies', but that was before the days of the commuter and the week-end gardener.

Naturally I do not suggest that you introduce this lovely weed to your garden in one of its two wild forms, though town gardeners who want quick cover for the walls of an unpromising back patch could consider it more often. But the two common forms are worth distinguishing as each suggests a different train of thought.

The white-trumpeted, large-leaved climber is not a convolvulus at all; I will not bother you with its Latin name except to remind you that it is gay but scentless. The smaller field bindweed is a true convolvulus and makes that ash-green tangle of smaller leaves on roadsides or the edge of cornfields where its neater and flatter bindweed flowers show up brightly in late summer. They are the rose-pink and pink-and-white-striped decoration among

Above: *Viburnum opulus compactum*, small Guelder Rose. Birds ignore these good autumn berries. 5 ft × 4 ft; May flowering. Loves lime or chalk. Grows slowly from cuttings (same in May). No pruning.
Right: *Euryops evansii*. Small shrub, c. 9 in high. Hardy in gritty soil, open ground. Hates bad drainage. June flowering. Grows from cuttings quite easily. Worth cutting it back hard in third spring after planting. Otherwise it loses shape. Likes lime

Overleaf: *Eryngium giganteum*. Biennial, up to 4 ft; June–July. Seeds itself, and thus is perpetuated. Any dry sunny soil. Very conspicuous

120

dry couch-grass and small white daisies. They are not atrociously rampant. On sunny days when their flowers are fully opened it is worth kneeling down to smell them as they are scented of almonds.

Where, though, is convolvulus for any garden? In connoisseurs' catalogues, mostly, for the brothers and sisters of our field bindweed are little known, unpopular but extremely well behaved and very beautiful. I will tantalize you with two of them.

The finest is worth the small trouble of preserving it through cuttings taken each autumn and wintered away from the frost: the North African bindweed, *Convolvulus mauretanicus,* looks just as pretty at Sissinghurst in late June as it now does in the rock garden at Kew. Its season is long, especially in a warm summer, and its typical chalk-blue flowers are a distinctive colour which mixes well and always attracts interested comment. On top of a dry wall, for example, it would enjoy the sharp drainage and form a carpet some 2 feet wide, frost permitting: another home might be a pot or urn where it could fall over the edge and make a pleasant alternative to the usual ivy-leaved geraniums.

Plants for pots are one idea we can borrow from grand public gardens and use appropriately at home. I have already noted down the use of Saint Bruno's lily, a small white-flowered perennial of great merit, a rusty orange musk called *Mimulus glutinosus* and the possibility of small bushes of silver-grey leaves, such as a 9-inch-high South African shrub called *Euryops evansii*.

The latter brings me, once again, to bindweed's foreign cousins: there is a particularly pretty silver-leaved convolvulus called *cneorum,* after (I believe) a Spanish aristocrat. It must be treated with care, for winter wet and extreme cold will kill it. Try planting it in very gritty earth in a pan or grouping it in one of those shallow urns that are popular but so difficult to garden satisfactorily. It will then delight you with the pink flowers of a refined field bindweed and a 9-inch clump of startingly silver leaves. Troublesome, but eminently worthwhile. You can buy it, like most silver plants, from Ramparts Nursery of Colchester, Essex.

If these two continental convolvuli will bring the smaller-flowered bindweed safely and charmingly into the late summer garden, what of the big white twiner who takes so much time to poison and uproot? The equivalent, here, is the wonderful Morning Glory, still better known for the absurd outcry about the hallucinatory powers of its seeds than for the vibrant blue funnels of its flowers. Like the big white twiner it is not a bindweed but has a different Latin name, in this case *Ipomoea*. Visitors to the Mediterranean should not be diverted by memories of whitewashed walls smothered in blue Morning Glory; in England I think Morning Glory is best as a summer pot plant, sown under glass or in a warm kitchen in April, potted up one to a pot in May, then placed outdoors in June with a tripod of bamboo canes and wire or wire netting to encourage it out of a pot, which should be 5 inches wide or more.

Previous page, above: *Sorbus aria*, Whitebeam. 40 ft eventually by 25 ft. Leaf at its best in late April. More dank in summer, but spring redeems it. Likes lime, chalk.
Below: Rose Harrison's Yellow. American hybrid. Not too prickly, flowers only in late May. c. 3–4 ft × 3 ft. I love this rose, especially beside blue *Ceanothus*. Will root from cuttings. No suckers

Lonicera tellmanniana Hybrid honeysuckle, from Budapest. Actually prefers a shady wall. Flowers in July; easy from cuttings. Trim after flowering

Its fleshy roots respond to liquid manure; if fed too late in the summer it tends to leaf rather than flower. It must be stood in the sunniest place possible, both to keep its flowers open for their very brief life and to encourage buds to form. If the temperature stays as low as in the usual English July, the leaves will turn a sick yellow in disgust: Morning Glory is perhaps most dependable in a conservatory or glasshouse, though the years of poor returns outdoors are soon forgotten in a year like 1973.

Visiting the seaside, I thought how peaceful a seaside garden could be. Predictions of doom and disorder could be left to those who were not by the sea nor keen on gardening; I could escape the offshore wind behind a barrier of grey willows and enjoy the different rustles and surges of the breeze in the leaves of tall poplars and holm oaks, thinking how sensible men were when they used to hear oracles in the movement of large trees' leaves, not in columns of ambiguous figures. We miss much by not listening attentively to the different sounds of hedges and tree trunks.

By the sea these tall barriers are especially important. Gardeners are at the mercy of fierce spring winds which whip across the garden and cut back the early spring shoots with their speed and their salt. Frost is not such a hazard, not least because seaside gardens are at sea-level and are seldom set in pockets which draw down frost: there is the temptation of growing tender plants on south-facing walls, limited only by the threat of these unpredictable winds. Even in East Anglia there are pomegranates trained on house walls, where they bear their pretty flowers of bright scarlet with a willingness which I must not allow to divert me. The only time I planted *Punica granata* I had it cut to the ground in its first winter. It was then trampled by a golden retriever who landed on the only shoot which came up after the cold.

Seaside gardeners are also up against sand. Of all the most coveted effects of nature, sand seems to me the most overvalued. Any town which can only boast a sandy beach deserves to turn into a resort: sand blows into my hair, clothes, lunch, eyes, blisters and gets up a baby's nose or into its bottle until I wonder why any parent ever becomes romantic about sandcastles or a trail of small footprints over the beach. In the garden it will root cuttings and drain clay but it is not very useful for much else. There are plants which will grow satisfactorily in sand, but not very many which prefer it.

The theme of a seaside garden could well be silver, because silver and grey leaves are one of the few attractions, apart from asparagus, which are happier on quick-draining sand. Wet is more of an enemy to them than cold. The silvering and furriness of a leaf is mostly nature's way of lessening a plant's loss of water and absorption of heat on a summer day. On quick-draining sand this silver barrier is a help in retaining the little water that stays in the soil.

So at tree level I would begin with two admirable but seldom planted grey-leaved trees, the grey willow *(Salix alba sericea)* and the silver poplar, *Populus candicans,* which looks such a picture of pure movement in our hedgerows when the wind ruffles the underside of its leaves. Both trees, especially the willow, can be kept to a height of about 6 feet by very hard pruning in spring and mid-summer; we should all use this trick more often on trees whose leaf-colouring we like, as they can then be included in the border or the small garden as shrubs with interesting leaves throughout the season.

The willow and poplar do have wider-spreading roots and in some areas the taller blue-grey cricket bat willow *(Salix caerulea)* would be preferable to the 20-foot-high grey willow. Neither can be lightly included as shrubs in a competing border of delicately rooted plants.

At the next level, the seaside shrub, I would unreservedly plant sea buckthorn *(Hippophae rhamnoides)* for its silvery leaf and its crop of orange-yellow autumn berries, produced by marrying one male to a bunch of females. Write to a nurseryman aware of the pitfalls of a plant's sex, such as Treseder's of Truro, Cornwall, until he supplies you with males as well as females; you will not need very many as they grow to a height of 15 feet and form trunks which remind me more of the sacred olive tree than anything else hardy in Britain. As their name implies, they do like to be beside the sea; the silvery-leaved sea purslane *(Atriplex halimus)* makes a splendid accompaniment and grows to a height of 6 or 7 feet, forming the sort of hedge which would never be dull in any light.

Enough, for the moment, of a silver frame for the seaside: as an evergreen contrast of a juicy fleshiness I would be free with a shrub called *Griselinia littoralis,* not (in my garden) hardy for very long inland, but particularly enviable in its variegated form near the seaside where it has just the right feel of lush permanence. Its Latin second name means 'of the shore', so again you cannot go far wrong with it. Artemisias, especially *splendens* and Lambrook Silver, and helichrysums, especially *fontainesii* and *petiolatum,* would spread round it, and no silver garden by the seaside can ignore them.

I would mass a silver sea holly, or eryngium, among them, none better than *giganteum,* a biennial which seeds abundantly and is my candidate for the most ignored easy plant in England. Its thistle-heads of grey-blue stand 3 feet tall among spiny silver-green leaves: it is also known as Miss Willmott's Ghost, Miss Willmott being a former plantswoman of the home counties with a tongue, and tastes, as sharp as a thistle's spine.

Sand suggests, besides silver, the Scots Burnet roses and I mention these easy and free-suckering shrubs because I have yet to see one in a seaside garden for which they are so suited. Any rose in the shrub section of *rugosa* or *spinosissima* origin will thrive in the sand of seaside gardens, a soil which so ill suits the far more familiar hybrid tree.

Prickly, I grant you, but bushes of that similar hybrid, the small Harrison's Yellow, will not sucker where you do not want

them; the scented white Blanc Double de Coubert, the velvety rose-purple Roseraie de l'Hay and the prolific pink Sarah van Fleet are three *rugosa* roses which would mass beautifully on sandy soil beneath my suggested curtain of silver. They are also three of my favourite roses, and the more I think of the range I can try, the more the September mood takes me and I feel that, wind or no wind, I must garden once by the sea before I die.

For the many gardeners who write and ask me for a specimen tree for a field or garden, I can think of few finer recommendations than the whitebeam; their variety is quite surprising, and their excellence is almost beyond dispute. Almost, I say, because there are still many gardeners to whom flower is more urgent than leaf and as the beauty of the whitebeam is its leaves, it is sometimes rejected as being too dull.

Now for those who plant only one kind of whitebeam, there is a half-truth in this. *Sorbus intermedia,* or the Swedish whitebeam, is a very pleasant tree, round-headed, about 20 feet high, widely available, and covered in tough green leaves which have a furry grey-green back to them. This fairly insignificant fur is the nearest the Swedish whitebeam comes to being white.

Attentive collectors of our own native whitebeam have now put this Swedish variety out of date. The magnificent *Sorbus aria lutescens* makes a big, wide-headed tree eventually, and in late April and May it is as colourful as any tulip and far more original than a pink suburban cherry. Its unfolding leaves are silvery white on their upper sides and so pronounced is their colour that in early summer the whole tree has a fresh gleam to it. This shining white fades with age and the passing of early summer, until the leaves settle down to a sober but polished green with only a hint of light on their grey undersides. By autumn, the whitebeam looks tired and ready to fall. It colours a little, yellow or red-brown, and then sinks back to a bare head of branches for winter.

This lovely tree needs room for its eventual width. It is a native in many parts of the country, though this *lutescens* sort is a selected form. For farmers who not only have enough of a social conscience to keep their hedgerows but also wish to beautify them, a line of whitebeams would be a magnificent complement to the firm shape of field maples *(Acer campestre)*. Like the maple, the whitebeam is a native on chalk soil, and the chalk flora are my favourite of all the various combinations this country offers. However, a whitebeam will also flourish in other less chalky sites and its resistance to seawinds, inland gales, urban filth, industrial belch and all-round cold is very high.

Other varieties have other merits. Uncommon forms of our *Sorbus aria* can be hunted out, a pretty weeping one called *pendula* which is said not to exceed 10 feet, a bigger-leaved one called *majestica* which is less silver-grey and so, to my mind, less interesting, and one which I could not resist including in a larger planting called *chrysophylla,* which flummoxed me the first time a botanist friend produced a twig of it, but in fact is a gay yellow-

Rose Blanc Double de Coubert, a *rugosa* rose. 5 ft × 4 ft. July–September. Excellent, too, on sandy soil. Light pruning in late autumn, if at all. Pretty yellow autumn leaf. Easy from July or autumn cuttings. Outstandingly good value

leaved whitebeam, a true curiosity, which is, however, a showy tree in its own right.

The name Sorbus, you may have realized, means that whitebeams are relations of our brightly-berried mountain ash. It is possible to have both the silver young leaf of the whitebeam and the autumn berries of the Sorbus family by planting the stately Himalayan Sorbus named *cuspidata,* a broad tall tree of distinction whose fruits are like brown marbles, and whose leaves are a good strong shape, especially silvered in a form called *sessilifolia.* By the landowner, this is a tree to be prized for its double attractions, but the modest gardener need not despair. Breeders have produced a small variety to suit his cramped surroundings. *Sorbus hybrida* (which is known, I believe more correctly, as *thuringiaca)* takes on an upright fastigiate form like a pillar and gives you red fruits and long grey-green leaves without branching outwards and shading the whole of your house.

Why are flowers scented? I was asking myself lately as I enjoyed the opportunity of suggesting plants for beds round a public seat. The immediate problem was the shortage of sweet-smelling flowers with which to stay the local councillors from their duties during late summer. Buddleias are too sickly: a perennial sweet thistle is too insignificant and apart from tobacco plants I was being driven to consider several rare hebes which the dictionaries said smelt 'appreciably'. One of the clearest divisions between gardens in August and gardens from winter till the fading of the first roses is this matter of smell. In winter sweet-scented flowers are almost the only flowers open; in late summer there are butterflies, fermenting apples and the season's leakage of oil smoking sharply on a tired mowing machine. So I wondered what I would have to do to deserve a scent if I was turned into a summer flower.

It would all depend, I find in my botany books, on my attar. Before you joke about Mother Nature scenting roses attar stroke, I remind you that attar is a Persian word meaning smell and that it applies to a plant's essential oil. This oil is puzzling, hence the word 'essential' to scare off further inquiry; it is also said to be secreted, another metaphor to put you off the scent. But the first points about it are easy enough.

Attar is stored in leaves and petals, not in a plant's sexual parts, and is released by evaporation. The cooler the air, the more gradually it evaporates, one reason for the richer smell of night-scented stocks in gardens after dark, and (I imagine) winter iris and winter sweet in chilly January. Lush petals which feel like velvet are slow to lose drops of attar, hence velvety roses do smell more gorgeous, quite apart from our romantically natured noses. Double flowers have more petals, hence more attar, which they also lose less rapidly.

From here on it is very much a question of explaining a familiar quality in terms of equivalent but unfamiliar chemistry. Attar is secreted as a waste mixture of sugar and oil, usually an alcoholic oil; alcohol is still used by scent makers to dissolve the chemicals of scent. This delicious sort of refuse is piled up because of the plant's chlorophyll, the magic green mixture behind so much plant growth whose origins and nature I cannot discuss here. Chlorophyll piles up sweet-scented oils in so far as it is not impeded by the pigment in a petal's colouring. This is a text-book fact which gardeners have to take on trust, for it explains more effects than it confuses. Heavily-pigmented flowers such as scarlet tulips or orange Super Star roses have very little smell because their colour hinders chlorophyll's part in producing attar. White flowers have no pigment, so a white garden of lilies, cream-white honeysuckle and rose Blanc de Coubert is not just an illogical exercise in upper-class taste.

There are two lines to the inquiry at this point. Either we can explore the chemicals and discuss the scent of mock orange blossom, my favourite summer scent, in terms of methyl anthranilate. Or we can ask whether plants have a reason for storing waste oils in the first place. These questions of function and design have always been dangerous. Our great-grandfathers used to dodge them by answering in terms of God's will, and now that ecology has become a cult, we answer in terms of some mystical balance of nature. The reasons for scent concern insects and pollination, but they cannot explain how the two matched themselves so neatly together. When I consider the only available reasons I am happy to think that their match was divine.

Flowers, like businessmen, suit their scent and appearance to the presumed preferences of their clients. Hawthorn smells of stale dung and wears a brown look on its white flowers in order to attract dung flies; moths go for the clove-scent of night-flowering campion which is released only when the air temperature falls below 45°F, usually, therefore, at night in its summer flowering season when moths are on the wing, able to pick out a pale colour like this campion's pale pink. Perhaps moths are common, too, in winter in the home countries, usually eastern ones, of the scented shrubs of a winter garden.

Bees are an exception to this rough rule, for they do not visit scents so much as colours, although they do not see colours as we do; they prefer blue and purple flowers but they see them more in terms of purple and red. White, to a bee, has a yellow suffusion, though how any scientist knows this for sure without being bee-minded himself I really cannot say.

So the answer to my question concerns moths, oils and fertility. As with flowers, so too with leaves; the resinous scent of the Mediterranean *maquis* which I covet for my own garden serves to deter grazing animals; the oils of thyme and rosemary leaves are strongly antiseptic and kill off germs. The sequence, if any, of these effects is more of a puzzle; which came first, the pungency of sage leaves or the browsing goat? When I smell lily of the valley I do not have to be a moth at nightfall to wish to believe that nature had planned it all from the start.

If ever you want to know what complaints your plants can cure, you should borrow the old herbals from a library. Among the herbalists, there is none more entertaining than John Gerarde (1597) or more voluminous than John Parkinson (1629 and thereafter). As Parkinson usually disagrees with Gerarde, that makes them more fun. On the hardy cyclamen, they are in their element. Gerarde begins by saying that 'men of good credit' have told him that the cyclamen grows wild on the hills of Wales and Lincolnshire, and in Somersetshire; also upon a fox-burrow not far from Master Bamfield's farm.

Charming though his geography is, it seems he may have been mistaken (he often was). For sixty years later, Parkinson said that he had very curiously inquired of many whether or not the cyclamen grows wild in England and they had all affirmed that they had never seen it and that it did not. Nowadays, there are a few naturalized clumps of the *neapolitanum* variety in the south, but most probably they have escaped from gardens. As this name shows, they belong in Italy near Naples.

But Gerarde has more to say. Cyclamen is known to him, as to some people now, by the English name of sowbread: in parts of Greece, indeed, it is still used as a food for pigs. This is one example where those fanatics, like Ruskin, who want to change all Latin plant names back to their coy English equivalents do not have right on their side. Cyclamen refers, presumably, to the spiral shape of the stem after flowering, as *kuklos* is the Greek for circle, a prettier idea than pigfood.

But back to herbals. Apart from feeding sows, cyclamen (hot and dry in the third degree) should be beaten into little flat cakes and is then 'a good amorous medicine to make one in love if it be inwardly taken'.

Poor old Parkinson obviously tried it as he found that 'as for its amorous effects, they are mere fabulous'. He was not using the word in its modern exclamatory way: he just meant they were stuff and nonsense. Certainly, he was never happily married. Had he been so, he might still have kept cyclamen in the cupboard. Anything said by the classical authors was treated with excessive respect by the sixteenth century's naturalists, and plants were no exception. It so happens that the Roman Pliny, who wrote wildly about many flowers, remarked in passing that cyclamen were useful for childbirth.

Gerarde is quickly on to this. Not only has his wife had 'great success in placing cyclamen leaves on the secret parts of women in travaile', but he himself was taking no chances in his garden. For so strong is the pull of cyclamen leaves on a woman with child that he had to counter their natural virtue by 'fastening sticks in the ground and others also crossways over them lest any visiting women should by lamentable experiment find my words to be true by stepping astride the said cyclamen and delivering long before their day'.

If you buy hardy cyclamen from a good nursery – there is a wide selection at Ingwersen's, Gravetye Nursery, East Grinstead, Sussex, or J. A. Mars, Haslemere, Surrey – you will be faced with the choice of whether to buy the corms dry or green and potted up. The potted sort are undoubtedly the easier to establish but they are more expensive. For those of you who want to economize, I would like to give some hints on planting the dry corms.

The danger is that you will plant them upside down. Not long ago I was potting up some rare fritillaries and I faced the same difficulty. The whole surface of the bulb was cracked and wrinkled like an old man's skin and what books like to call basal roots seemed to have been sprouting in all four directions. In the end I trusted to luck and hoped that the young shoots would right themselves if I was wrong. But cyclamen, often, will not right your mistakes. Their dry shapes are just as perplexing.

I will take the most common variety, *neapolitanum*, first. This flowers from August onwards and its pink bent-back flowers are very well known. I do, however, urge you to try the selected white variety too as this is more lovely. Remember that this variety roots from the top of the corm, unlike a normal garden plant. This is not much help unless you know which side is the top: the test here is a negative one, for the surface which is hollowed out in a concave way is the bottom. The whole corm looks saucer-shaped, so all you have to do is to look for the broad hollow and plant your cyclamen resting on that. On no account be misled by cracks or dents that are not concave hollows; they belong on the top, facing uppermost.

Cyclamen neapolitanum. September flowering. The easiest, even among tree- or hedge-roots

And do not panic at the sight of last year's roots and then abandon my advice and put them face downwards. As I say, they are perverse and like to be on top. No hardy cyclamen likes to be deeply planted. A 2-inch covering above the corm is quite enough. Often a huge old corm will rise to the surface like a gnarled old fish coming up for air, amaze you with its girth – often 6 inches across – and still produce its 3-inch-high flowers quite happily.

Far and away the best time to plant *neapolitanum* and indeed any other variety is early July, when they are all but dormant. Always handle the dry corms very carefully. If you tip them out of the packet and plant them where they fall, thinking you are being more natural that way, you will probably break the little surface roots that matter most.

Neapolitanum has lovely flowers. They always remind me of Ernest Shepherd's drawing of Piglet in a high wind, with his ears streaming out horizontally behind him, like a cyclamen flower laid on its side. They also smell good in warm weather and from October till April the marbled green leaves are a fine carpet. When the flowers are over, their stems coil down flat against the earth as if they were taking a bow. They are full of seed which is worth saving. If you sow it at once and leave the pots out in winter to freeze there is a strong chance that it will sprout. But you need patience before they reach flowering size and patience is not a plant that grows in every man's garden. If you leave the seed alone, it often germinates beside the parent. Sometimes cyclamen spread far and wide, helped by ants who convoy the seed between

Above left: *Cyclamen repandum*. Flowers in late spring, more or less hardy, but even better in a cold house or frame

Below left: *Cyclamen graecum*. Summer flowering, best in very dry place in sun or else in a pot. Likes lime, as do all others

Below: *Cyclamen coum alpinum*. Late winter, early spring. Hardy. Will grow in full sun

their front feet. Incredibly, *neapolitanum* revels in dry shade and is happy among the roots of huge old trees. I wish public parks would try it there. It loves lime; if you want to hurry it into flower, give it water in August. I have never known it do well in very built-up city areas. This is its disadvantage.

Neapolitanum alone is good enough but there are many other varieties, some not quite hardy, which are just as lovely and prolong the season almost the whole year round. *Coum*, *atkinsii* and *hiemale* flower in mid-winter, gallantly. *Repandum* is in full glory in April. *Libanoticum*, *pseud-ibericum* and my favourite *persicum* are all special. They are slightly tender, so they are safer in a pot in a cold house. *Graecum* is often out by July, *europaeum* is excellent in August.

That last paragraph is almost more Latin than English but each of those names refers to a very individual beauty. Each has its idiosyncrasies, like an old lady, and I like them all. I would need a hundred tongues to describe them or complain how the florists have blown up the *persicum* varieties into those huge pot plants we give out at Christmas. The real *persicum* has long reflexed petals of blush-white with a dark spot at their base: it smells deliciously and flowers in March. I do beg you to try it in gritty, limy earth in a shallow pan. It takes up little room and unlike its forced, waxy children, I have never known it wilt within a week and die. It comes from Rhodes and Cyprus, the drier hillsides of Asia and the sparse slopes of inner Iran. Fern and a surfacing of florist's moss are far from the nature of this lovely wild flower.

Families of garden plants are even more entangled and extensive than those of a village or an aristocracy; Rothschilds are as nothing before the ranunculi and their relations, while an accurate peerage of roses and their family members would take more hours of pedantry than a guide to every family in Cornwall.

The connections of garden plants were nicely brought home to me recently by several inquiries. First, a man wrote about his hedgerows in Cambridgeshire. Chalky soil, he said, as wind-swept as a precipice, and in need of some strong specimen trees. Never mind if they were not evergreen, but for the sake of the landscape, he would prefer them to be of one kind, agreeing that too many different varieties in succession can seem restless.

I suggested, on a whim, our common field maple. Probably he snorted and dismissed it as too ordinary, but this is a native tree for which I have an extraordinary fondness. Its shape is very decisive, as if it knows its place in the plant world and is determined to take its stand there. It is round headed, a sturdy 20 feet high, and graciously equipped with five-lobed leaves. It is often to be seen as a young bush, encroaching on a crab-apple tree or competing with the Traveller's Joy which enlivens our hedgerows even in November, smothering them with its greying seedheads as if a flock of sheep had left their wool on the brambles underneath.

The field maple, or *Acer campestre*, will put up with any cold

Acer griseum, Paperbark Maple. 15–30 ft. Quite bright in autumn, but best for bark. Will grow on lime. Not to be propagated by amateurs

wind on a chalky soil. As a native plant, it has chosen to grow in Britain of its own accord. We are often unfair to what our own flora offers us: in the old imperial gardens of Schloss Schonbrunn, in Vienna, there is a magnificent hedge of our field maple, thick, regular and beautifully matured. In a grand setting, on limy soil, it would be fitting and rewarding to plant a future rival in England.

Next enquiry came, I would guess, from one of the few young couples who have recently found a first home with as much room and grounds as they wanted; they did not mind waiting forty years for results, but they wanted a specimen tree for their lawns (revealing plural, thought I), and as she had been interested in botany at school, he would like something unusual, not so much for its flowers but perhaps for its leaf or bark.

Snakebarks, I thought to myself, not realizing the link, and pictured their future children prising off bits of this striped bark as a trophy, or simply as something to pass the time; the best, unfortunately, is also the most difficult to increase, as its seeds are extremely erratic and it cannot be grafted easily. But *Acer griseum*, a maple again, is a most original small tree. After some seventy years away from its native China its oldest specimens in England are said to be about 40 feet high, and it is for their straight trunks that gardeners love them, although their red autumn leaves are also very fine. They are not so much striped in their bark as torn and tattered. One season's bark hangs in huge flakes, like sunburnt skin, and peels back to reveal the young, orange bark underneath. This does not sound as appealing as it looks, for *Acer griseum* is more a flakebark than a snakebark. If you would rather have a striped effect on your tree trunk, I recommend you to *Acer davidi,* a fellow Chinaman, or otherwise to the less vivid *Acer capillipes*. Both of these are marked by long vertical threads of white in their bark. As the tree grows these become more and more prominent. Neither is difficult to please, and as specimens for larger gardens no young man of property should ignore them.

A third enquiry was different again. A lady from Dorset wanted a lightly coloured shrub for a dark and slightly shaded woodland situation. Rounding off my trio, I could not resist suggesting an *Acer* again. From Japan, we now can enjoy the coral-barked maple, or *Acer palmatum* Senkaki, and even if this shrub needs protection from winter winds and the late spring frosts which savage its young leaves, it is unmistakable among maples.

Eventually, it will form a small and rather upright tree in favourable west country gardens, but I like it in its youth when its fresh and pale leaves of Lincoln green are as graceful as any other of the cut-leafed maples. Senkaki also has vivid stems of coral pink, like a warmer dogwood, and retains this colour throughout the winter. In the autumn, its leaves turn a gentle orange before falling, and so Senkaki, despite its awful name, is indeed a shrub for all seasons. Best, however, in milder gardens, such as that of my fortunate Dorset lady.

Three requests for three different problems, and yet each could be answered honestly by recommending an acer. Maples, maybe, are on my brain at the moment, but their varied merits are a reminder of the surprising range which can be found by gardeners who do not rest satisfied with only one member from each family of garden plants.

As gardeners mostly complain that their gardens grow too slowly, I have been considering how to plant a garden for the quickest results. Annuals and other summer plants from seed are the most obliging choice, supported by bulbs of all kinds, except perhaps the snowdrop which has a way of refusing to flower or spread for several years after it has been moved. But these bulbs and annuals have no solidity.

A garden should be more than a brightly coloured hayfield: trees, evergreen cover and shrubs with firmly shaped leaves are needed to stiffen it up. The finest trees, like the finest leaves and evergreens, are suspected of being too slow for most of our climate, so I have tried to think up a few alternatives.

Among trees, foresters are beginning to realize the merits of a cousin of the beech tree called nothofagus. I have seen this planted commercially in Ireland as an experiment in speed, yet English nurseries rarely list it and gardeners on the acid soil which it likes show little interest in all it can offer. These southern beeches grow wild in New Zealand and South America, especially Chile, and are a last reminder that the two continents were once joined together in their prehistory. Like many plants from the southern hemisphere, the southern beeches will grow extremely fast, pacing a Lombardy poplar in gardens which are free of lime and sheltered from wind. Their leaves are small, like a small beech or hornbeam, and their autumn colouring is most remarkable: each leaf changes individually to its own shade of orange, red, brown or plain green, so that the upright shape of the tree looks unusually like a patchwork.

The shape of a southern beech is not particularly attractive, for fast growth gives it an upright and slightly scrawny appearance. Nor is the Antarctic variety recommended for sites which need a tree, as it divides into several trunks and turns into a shrub with twisting stems; no doubt this is a protection against the winds of its exposed home. But a Chilean variety called *obliqua* is rapid, upright and much to my liking. In twenty years' time, a forester tells me, it will be at least 70 feet high. Quite a monument, then, to plant, even when you first draw your pension.

Among Antipodean trees, of course, none is faster than the eucalyptus, a species which is being trusted more than ever by trade growers to overtake our threatened shortage of pulp and paper. Its many varieties can be grown easily from seed and will seem tree-like by their third year: readers with a mild climate and an acre or two might well like to gamble on a eucalyptus plantation against the day when there is no paper for the public. There is always the oil too, from the leaves, though my favouite variety is called *citriodora* and smells of lemon, less useful to the trade.

All eucalyptus can be grown cheaply and very quickly from seed. It is a waste to buy them as shrubs.

Poplars, naturally, you all know, though I do exhort all planters of alleys, walks and edgings of drives to consider the scented balsalm poplar no stranger to my recommendations. Balsalm poplar seduces by its name alone, and this is indeed a delightful tree for an avenue because its young leaves give off a pleasantly tempered scent of the sort of balsam that children are made to sniff under towels when they have bad colds. The sticky leaf-buds are too pungent if you handle them, but alongside a walk to a house or a spinney, they waft their sweetly resinous smell on any warm wind, particularly after the rain.

Only eight years are needed to turn them from saplings into a tall avenue. There are very few difficulties about their life, except that they resent particularly heavy soil: commercially, I believe, they too are in demand for matches and pulp after five or six years of growth, and it is possible for the grander sort of smallholding to be given a grant towards a whole grove of balsam poplars, provided the owner is prepared to see them cut early and sold. This is not too regrettable for a balsam copse, for a very important reason which I must explain. Though slender-trunked, the balsam poplars do most of their work underground. They have long and wide-ranging roots, more than 10 yards from their stem, and they are very powerful. I have known a screen of balsams unsettle a surfaced tennis court, while one in a London garden is making a bold assault on a house-wall.

At maturity, an age at which they are seldom seen, they are very tall, three-storied like a high French Gothic cathedral. If you can think big, a balsam every four or five yards will make an avenue of which you can be proud. Be sure to choose the form known as *balsamifera*, not the far less scented *candicans* (*tacamahaca* is also excellent, and I hear well of the Chinese *szechuanica* too). If you know a balsam avenue, simply take long cuttings, 3 or 4 feet high, embed half their length in the ground and you will find that they root delightfully easily. If you cannot wait for a mature shrub, choose a tree, after some thought, and cut it hard whenever it tries to grow out of reach. There is a wide choice here which gardeners have hardly begun to sample.

I was reading recently the plans of the great Miss Jekyll, mistress of Munstead Wood and the modern garden, and I noticed how she advised the hard pruning of plane trees, especially the golden-leaved plane tree, for places at the back of her wide borders. The result, leading to larger and richer leaves, would be most unusual: it could be repeated with the catalpa, a favourite tree with town gardeners, the golden catalpa, sea buckthorn, cornel trees, the Stag's Horn sumach (*Rhus typhina*), the silver poplar, willows (and not only the brilliant red-twigged willows for winter), the golden-leaved Honey Locust tree called *Gleditschia* Sunburst, a lovely new variety which even outdoes the new golden acacia with its similar but lesser leaf. Finest of all is the half-hardy

Paulownia, which bears really huge leaves like hairy green hand-kerchiefs if it is cut to within a foot of the ground in spring. This is another tree which is cheaply and copiously available from seed, supplied from the huge list of Thomson and Morgan, Ipswich, Suffolk. I have already praised the Tree of Heaven for the same purpose.

Impatience, then, is only a matter of thoughtlessness in many prominent places in the garden. I will not say that a plane tree, heavily pruned, is the equal of a slow Chinese magnolia, but it is four times as quick to fill its space. It has often been remarked that men are most prone to plant trees when they are getting old: if the ageing tree-planter were to cut his trees back every year after planting, he would not leave a memorial to outlast him, but he would enjoy the equal of a fast-growing shrub, to the envy of others who have chosen more conventionally.

My favourite climbers are not particularly quick about their job, but as few books or lists are honest about the relative speed of climbing plants I will also set down a few of the fastest for your purpose. Quick growth, of course, depends on site and climate, like most other qualities in the garden. But there are some broad divisions which are true throughout the country.

The Russian vine (listed as *Polygonum baldschuanicum* after a Russian, I imagine) is familiar enough and its light sprays of pearl-white flowers are not objectionable. This is an extremely rampant plant, only to be used in cases of deep despair or designs by Basil Spence. It will jam up the gutters and grow under the tiles of most low cottage roofs where impatient gardeners plant it and regret it within two years. But the Russian vine will also grow from a London basement below the street to the eaves of a three-storied house. It is shy, however, if planted in a tub and left on a hard surface, unless the tub is watered heavily and very frequently. I have always hoped to live where I would not need this climbing knotweed, but many gardeners have to be grateful to it.

A less common alternative is the Chinese gooseberry, very quick indeed on a west or warmer wall. Where the Russian vine smothers with a curtain, this rapid climber sprawls with long feelers and grows rapidly to a height of 20 feet. It has to be held in position with wires and this may put you off it, but its bold leaves and hairy stems are far more impressive than a Russian vine's. In August there is a faint but pleasing scent from yellow-white flowers which fade to buff-yellow, like a honeysuckle's, when they are fertilized. Fruits follow, like elongated gooseberries. The Chinese gooseberry's Latin name is *Actinidia chinensis,* far more rampant than its pink, white and green-leaved cousin. A well-stocked nursery like Notcutt's, of Woodbridge, in Suffolk, can supply it.

If you insist on an evergreen for a particularly hideous wall, there is none more dependable than the Japanese honeysuckle, *Lonicera japonica halliana,* which gives good cover by its third year. Those who want maturity, evergreen or not, in their first season will have to content themselves with the half-hardy

Above left: *Cyclamen persicum.* Spring flowering. Best in a cold house or cold frame. Not safe outdoors, but easy, scented and the most beautiful of cyclamens

Below left: *Acer davidi.* Small tree with striped bark; any deep soil. Some autumn colour

Above right: *Acer griseum* and *Ceratostigma plumbaginoides.* The latter flowers September–October, about 6 in high, slow to establish, then very quick to spread. Sometimes it bears more stems than flowers, but in a dry limey soil it can be excellent. Very bright autumn colour. Very easily increased from its running stems. Not for small rock gardens

Below right: *Rhus typhina,* the Stag's Horn sumach

Overleaf: *Paulownia tomentosa.* Grows to 30 ft, wide spreading. In very warm years will flower as a tree in May. Best pruned hard to base in April–May to encourage big leaves, vigorous to height of 6 ft. Fairly hardy, but likes to avoid worst frost. Very easy indeed from seed

Cobaea, grown as an annual and planted outdoors in early June. This astonishingly quick grower will remove a reasonably sunny wall or trellis from view by mid-August. Although it will not survive frost it can be most usefully grown between and above slower climbers for their first two or three years. Seed of the preferable white variety can be bought from Thompson and Morgan of Ipswich.

Other annual climbers such as the yellow canary creeper and the scarlet eccremocarpus are quite pretty in a warm summer, but are several speeds and thicknesses behind cobaea, at least in England. Hops, however, are another blessing for the impatient man, especially in their variegated forms. Like cobaea they should be grown one each to a pot and planted out in late May when well up their bamboo cane. The Golden Hop is the brightest.

The test for all quick-growers is whether or not they look presentable before the middle of their third season after planting. Often the most rampant plants are the slowest to seem established, like a small so-called plumbago *(Ceratostigma larpentae)* which crept miserably for six years before deciding to run wild over two square yards of my surrounding alpine plants. The pink and white forms of *Clematis montana,* ivies of all kinds, evergreen garrya for green winter catkins, climbing hydrangeas, so lovely now when its leaves are turning clear yellow, these familiar 'quick' climbers accelerate, in my experience, only after three years.

Single roses with wild Oriental blood or rambling kinds like Wedding Day, Albertine, Alberic Barbier and Pauls Scarlet have left behind the more elegant and shapely kinds like Guinee or even Mermaid by the time the third year turns. Virginia creeper, usually, is quick off the mark, though the most reliably rampant vine I have found to be the big-leaved *Vitis coignetiae* which is a compulsory choice for a bare wall in a town garden, not least for its flame-purple autumn colouring.

This business of speed will limit your choice of quality and will certainly disappoint you if you do not consider what I call the three-year rule. But if you want a cover and you cannot wait, you could do worse than copy nature: all through our hedgerows on limy soil the wild *Clematis vitalba* or Travellers' Joy is about to round off its season of pale green flower and leaf with that wonderful show of fluffy seed-heads. I put this climber first for gardeners with no patience, yet they seldom plant it. In the hurry to have a full-grown garden, we do not even stop to look for Travellers' Joy beyond the garden wall.

A garden is a place to sit in, never more so than in the sunny autumn weather which is becoming an English tradition. The search for a sensible garden seat is never easy, and I can only recommend you to some private carpentry to make a low bench seat of the style which we showed, most pleasantly in my opinion, in two of the gardens which the *Financial Times* laid out at the Chelsea Flower Show. It was a rectangle surfaced with wooden

Cobaea scandens. Half-hardy climber; flowers August–September. Rampant; good in towns or on half-shaded walls. Sow in early March under glass and grow on in pots till June. Very easy

slats which could be painted or blackened with creosote. If you want a useful feature to be inconspicuous in the landscape you should consider painting it black or dark green in order to conceal it. Our bench seat was fitted round a tree trunk, a square hole allowing it to sit snugly round the trunk's diameter.

Its upper surface could have been hinged and the sides blocked in to make a large box in which to store tools, toys and flowerpots. The box's lid would be the seat. This bench design could also run along the foot of a wall in a small town garden where the horizontal line of the slats on its surface would help to draw the eye along the garden's length. It is a neater and more effective design than those frilly white-painted pub seats which have suddenly sprung into fashion and which I urge you to ignore.

Suppose, then, you have found a seat which is comfortable, unlike those chilly stone antiques which are useless for most self-respecting bottoms. How are you to plant round it? For scent, surely, as there are few higher pleasures than sitting on a seat and smelling the flowers. Yet I seldom find a seat with a sweet-smelling plant very near it. I do not suggest you plant a small aromatic plant like peppermint or thyme actually on the seat's surface, in a pocket of soil, as has sometimes been recommended for those who wish to crush out a sweet smell as they sit down. Bees do visit these plants and their leaves will not stand a repeated squashing. But there are other alternatives.

Evergreen shrubs would be welcome, for there is little joy in sitting down to look at bare twigs in springtime. My favourite, the tubular white flowered *Osmarea burkwoodii,* can even be clipped to give a dark leathery-green recess to the seat behind which it is planted in a thicket. Its flowers are open in April or May and can be accompanied by the yellow flowering currant, *Ribes aureum,* unfamiliar brother of those smelly dark red varieties which are so popular for difficult corners. This ribes has a small tubular golden flower and is scented extremely sweetly of spice and vanilla, at least to my nose. Allow it to grow up to 6 feet tall and wide: you can multiply it quickly by cuttings and you may agree that its rounded and indented leaf is charming. Not, however, an evergreen, and for this I would look back to two earlier winter shrubs.

One, the golden-leaved *Daphne odora aureo-marginata,* has been praised often enough already for you to know that it is mauve-pink flowered, hardy against a south wall, 3 or 4 feet high and the most heavenly scented shrub in this book. It will also, I find, grow well in a 7-inch pot and gritty earth kept up to the mark with liquid manure; in a pot you can move it indoors for safety during cold winters. Its companion could be the neglected Sarcococca whose evergreen leaves resemble the elegant Butcher's Broom and bear dull but very sweet greenish-white flowers in January.

Inside this frame of evergreens there would of course be room for rosemary, lavender and a bush of the dwarf philadelphus; also

Clematis vitalba, Travellers Joy or Old Man's Beard. Native chalk flora; easy from seed. No pruning unless it needs a thinning. Greenish flowers and fluffy seed-heads. Rampant

147

Ribes aureum, Yellow Flowering Currant. Up to 4 ft, spreading. April, scented flowers. Happy on any soil, very dense shade under trees. Easy from long cuttings after flowering

the incense rose called Primula whose stems smell of incense after a shower of rain. White regale lilies, perhaps in pots, lily of the valley in its Everest form, perhaps under the seat where it could live in the half-shade it enjoys: these sweet white flowers could combine with the woodruff called *Asperula odorata* which smells of hay, *Viburnum juddii*, a delicious May shrub, golden Lemon Balm to pinch, Thyme Silver Queen to bruise and perhaps an arch of the late Dutch honeysuckle overhead to lull you to sleep on midsummer evenings.

If there were a ledge nearby, perhaps from a wall, I would cover it with pots of scented autumn crocuses, especially one called *longiflorus;* lilac would have to be nearby both in its tubular Canadian varieties such as the pink Bellicent and in the more normal, but differently-scented forms such as Madame Lemoine. Pinks of all kinds, especially one called Bats Double which smells of cloves, catmint and variegated apple mint, a particularly fresh late summer plant, would round off the scent at ground level. All plants as smelly as broom, as sickly as white *Clematis montana* or as stale as hardy penstemons would be removed to a corner for appearances only.

So much, then, for a scented seat and I leave you to elaborate, remembering the night-scented stock and campion if you like to enjoy summer twilight in the open after dinner. There is a mass worth choosing according to your nose and fancy; the problem, as you can see from my suggestions, is to leave the sitter space in which to be seated.

November

On my way to work one morning I came across a pleasant surprise. Usually, it is the time of day when my thoughts are furthest from the garden. My route lies down a passage lined by classical sculpture. I turn right where the Emperor Augustus casts a provincial glance at his deceptively dainty wife on the opposite wall. I move between cases of Dark Age cutlery and turn left by two large Viking stones engraved with runic script. Until I happened to look behind the doorway, these museum surroundings had always depressed me.

Behind the door stood a gravestone of blue-black granite with a faded but familiar inscription. 'Know, stranger, ere thou pass, beneath this stone, lye JOHN TRADESCANT, grandsire, father, son . . .' A chain of happy memories was touched off by these words. In the history of English gardening, there are few more stirring names than the first two Johns of the Tradescants. I had always believed that their gravestone was still with their bodies, in the cemetery of St Mary's, Lambeth. But in the 1880s, it seems, it was rescued from ruin and presented to Oxford where the rest of the Tradescant mementoes, their fine family portraits and museum knick-knacks, had notoriously come to rest.

Gardeners today owe the Tradescants a permanent vote of thanks. In the early seventeenth century, they introduced England to a whole range of unknown flowers, most of which we now regard as part of the English garden. Through their travels, we first saw the lilac, the Dutch medlar, the passion flower, red dogwood, the evening primrose, the night-scented stock, one, if not both, of the parents of our London plane tree, the wild pomegranate, virginia creeper, Stag's Horn sumach, the so-called acacia and the tulip tree. That selection of their imports is enough to make the point: thanks to the Tradescants, the old Elizabethan gardens, relying very much on herbs and a limited range of flowers, could develop into gay variety during Charles's reign.

Though John the younger made a valuable visit to Virginia, it is John the elder who is my favourite. He came from a Suffolk family, was married in 1607 and died in 1638. But in between, the details of his life are irresistible. His big break had come by 1609 when he is recorded as an employee of the Cecil family at Hatfield, in the pay of the first Lord Salisbury, son of Queen Elizabeth's great counsellor. The gardens were more than enough to occupy him and from the family accounts, we have a vivid idea of his materials. His employer encouraged him to travel. In 1611, he was in Flanders and Paris, buying a mass of new plants, especially fruits, including 200 lime trees at half a crown each, 'flowers called anemone', many types of mulberry, medlars, quinces, one pot of gilliflowers (cost: nothing) and a very good brand of redcurrant. He was fast becoming a dab hand at growing melons; his taste for a lime avenue was in advance of his age and his fruit was the 'choicest for goodness and size'. The triangular walks, parterres, vines and deer fences at Hatfield passed his time most happily.

Robert Cecil was the perfect patron for the inquisitive gardener, supervising each new plan, sponsoring foreign travels and always extending his flowerbeds further into the park. He was also appreciative. On the grand staircase at Hatfield, he ordered John's picture to be carved, showing him pointing his toe and holding his rake in one hand and a basket of his new fruits in the other. But the best memorial is still in the account book: 'to John Tradescant, the poor fellow that goeth to London – 2s. 6d.' Every country gardener can sympathize with that.

From Hatfield, John moved on to Canterbury; from Canterbury he joined an expedition to Russia, keeping a careful diary of sea breezes and scenery as well as a charming section headed 'things by me observed'. His spelling throughout is frightful but his plant discoveries are most important, culminating in his introduction of the larch tree. In 1620, he sailed for seven months in the Mediterranean as part of a convoy against Barbary pirates, using the trip as an excuse to gather more new plants, whether pomegranates or Persian lilacs. Safely back in England, he was taken on by the Duke of Buckingham, planting another lime avenue for his benefit and then sailing off with his troops to the tiny island of Rhé to discover the night-scented stock and the scarlet corn poppy. John would have personally preferred the poppy as, on his own admission, he was incapable of detecting any niceties of smell – one reason, doubtless, why he revelled in growing fruits and was not satisfied with ordinary aromatic herbs.

In 1630 he received his crowning honour. He was appointed keeper of the Royal Gardens, Vines and Silkworms at Oatlands, serving Charles I and Henrietta Maria, the 'rose and lily Queen' as his tombstone charmingly puts it. His salary was £100 a year; he had become a man of property, owning a house dubbed The Ark in Lambeth, where he built up a famous collection of curiosities, from Russian vests to Barbary spurs, many of which he had found on his travels. These were later to form the core of Oxford's Ashmolean Museum, home of his fine bearded portrait and, as I found, the famous family tombstone.

We do have a tradescantia to commemorate the family, but its growth is disappointing. A prettier memorial lies in the words on the family gravestone:

> *Whilst they (as Homer's Iliad in a nut)*
> *A world of wonders in a closet shut . . .*
> *Transplanted now themselves, sleep here; and when*
> *Angels shall with their trumpets waken men*
> *And fire shall purge the world, these three shall rise*
> *And change this Garden then for Paradise.*

Tradescantia virginiana Iris Pritchard. c. 2 ft, herbaceous. Flowers June–July. Any sunny soil. Easily divided. Seedlings easy, but variable

Gardeners are always well advised to think before they plant, but they have to exercise their brains if they are gardeners without a garden. There is no contradiction in this. There are garden-

ers in fifth-floor flats, gardeners in caravans and even, so a man
reminds me by his questioning letters, gardeners on Persian Gulf
oil rigs. Nobody ever pays much attention to them and the
popular dictionaries which spring to my mind begin with instructions for making a compost heap, cutting a serpentine bed or
merely testing the soil with a bit of litmus paper. Not much use if
your only border is the border on your curtains and your only bed
the one you sleep in.

Please, even on the fifth floor, do not write gardening books off
as irrelevant. Living recently in London, I have been thinking
how I would get round an aerial existence if I ever had to put up
with one for long. Certainly, a gardener does not always need
earth. Every autumn windowsill could have its row of colchicums,
or giant autumn crocus, as long as it could support a row of
saucers, each with its bulb, with or without some water.

The results are not too awful, as long as you are wary of a
highly praised variety called Waterlily which is expensive and has
such monstrously double mauve flowers that it collapses at the
neck and leaves you with a tattered confusion of shapeless petals.
It reminds me of an emergent moth with muscle failure. I cannot

Right: *Colchicum speciosum album.* 9 in high tuber, flowers September. Mossy leaves in spring and early summer. Any soil, but leaves are said to poison livestock.

Left: *Phyteuma comosum.* Flowers in June; 3 in high. Likes lime, very sharp drainage; also best in tufa or gritty pan or sink. Smoked salmon to a slug; not difficult from seed

say that I like a colchicum as much as an autumn crocus and indeed I believe that the faultless common *Crocus speciosus* would produce its clear blue flowers quite happily without any soil, on a saucer too. I have had it in flower in paper bags, having bought it and failed to plant it in time. The yellow lily of the Biblical field, *Sternbergia lutea,* will also flower on a bare ledge. After one year, however, it is finished.

But as far as colchicums go, and their glossy green leaves do go an unfortunately long way in springtime, the white-flowered kind called *album* has always seemed to me to be the prettiest. Just stand it on your windowsill indoors in September and it will flower on last season's impetus. No earth is needed for it, and if you give it water after flowering, add a little liquid manure from time to time and tolerate its spring greenery, it will build up strength for a repeat performance next year.

It is surprising what you can grow with water. Propagators trapped in a town flat can enjoy rooting fuschias, hebes and other slightly tender shrubs with sappy growths, not to mention dog-woods, both red and yellow, ribes or flowering currant and skimmias, by putting autumn cuttings in a jam-jar full of water and waiting for them to throw out roots within a month. Quite what you do with a dogwood indoors, I am not yet certain, so perhaps you would rather try growing hyacinths in those water-glasses with a suitably broad top and narrow neck which any worth-while garden centre will supply for you.

155

Over the years my results have varied. The stringy white roots of the hyacinth always look very elegant through the glass as they coiled down into the water, but the flowers often fail to grow a stalk and come out stunted at the top of the bulb, even though I keep them in darkness to let them form roots. Otherwise they shoot up and then look top heavy. A hyacinth cannot be tied upright when it is balanced in a water glass and so I have tried to stand mine on top of a piano and pretend that they look like flowering candles at a jaunty angle. They never do, really, but the sight of their roots in water which I have sweetened with charcoal is pleasing for a while. The flowers are less important.

If a hyacinth in water is not enough to convert any flat-dwelling gardeners, let me tantalize them with orchids instead. The splendid pleiones do need some earth, but not very much. They are not very messy. They win prizes at alpine garden shows, yet they are seldom seen in gardening homes. They do have an exotic appearance, being 6 inches high when they bear their 4-inch-wide flowers of white or mauve-pink like a flatter and broader daffodil whose central trumpet is often flushed deeply or flecked with brown.

They flower generously in March and April. Their single leaf of pale ribbed green does not get in the way of their buds. They can be crammed six to a 5-inch pot of peat. Their pseudo-bulbs, available at a sane price in several forms from Broadleigh Gardens, Somerset, should not be buried when you plant them, preferably in December. They do not want any heat, though they do

Pleione limprichtii. 6 in high, 'bulbous' orchids; spring flowering. Very easy in pans. Possible outside, usually under pane of glass in winter. Likes peat, leaf mould, grit; little water in winter, plenty in spring and summer. Throws out young pseudo 'bulbs' which increase the stock

not object to it. Gardeners in the west country can grow them outside beneath a pane of glass to protect their flowers from mud and wind. I prefer them in a cool room where I can inspect them without a pane of glass to detract from them.

After flowering you gradually reduce their water until the leaf dies down. You are left with a blank pot of earth and often twice as many pleiones as when you began. Their merit is that they are happy in a shallow pan and do not need an ugly big pot. Unlike, say, an amaryllis they do not follow their flowers with sheafs of unmanageable leaves. *Formosana* is the easiest and cheapest mauve-pink variety: *limprichtii* is darker, costlier and very lovely, while Polar Sun is particularly well named if you have ever seen the mauve-white effect of early morning sun over the Arctic ice-packs.

Having noted the pleiones, or pink-mauve orchids, you should now be ready for the practice which surprises me more than any other in gardening. I mean the growing of plants in rock without any earth at all.

Mountain climbers will at once see how natural this is. Between the cliffs of the Dolomites or Engadine the fussiest alpine plants will often be found living on a diet of broken rubble and dust and forming tighter and smaller cushions because of their lack of food; this contentment, a lesson for us all, can be brought inside your house with the help of a stone called tufa. Tufa is a soft and porous sort of limestone which does not have to be chiselled; you simply saw it into small pieces like a gorgonzola cheese and then use a screwdriver or the like to bore holes in its surface for your alpine plants.

There are tufa outcrops in England and I am told of one in Derbyshire near Matlock and another near Wells in Somerset; tufa is also to be found in the crypt of Rochester Cathedral or else, for despairing gardeners whose builders' merchants cannot help them out, in the catalogues of W. E. Ingwersen Ltd, Gravetye Nurseries, East Grinstead, Sussex, where it is rather expensive. However, it is a very light rock indeed and a hundredweight of it will go a long way, so do not be deterred by the price of a load. Mostly, you are paying for transport.

In the raw, tufa is an unpleasant plaster-white which you will certainly want to soften to a natural honey-yellow: paint it over with sour milk and you will hasten the growth of mosses and a weathered coating of old age, but you must be careful not to block the entire stone with moss-greenery, for its surface is also to be your flowerbed. Tufa contains small pockets of air which will drain away water and give a cool run to the long roots of alpine plants; it is riddled with lime and with traces of useful chemicals such as magnesium. It needs no other food at all to grow you the finest alpine campanulas you have ever considered possible. Indeed, the most remarkable collection of rare alpine plants in this country is housed in an artificial cliff of tufa with a glass-paned roof overhead like an old conservatory; it is sited within a mile

Edraianthus pumilio.
Related to Harebells. Any
sunny soil; good on lime.
Flowers up to 6 in. Not
difficult from seed

of Birmingham's city centre and grows the hairiest and fluffiest
alpine androsaces and verbascums because it can offer them such
perfect drainage, even in an area that is far from smokeless.

A small weathered piece of tufa is extremely pretty in its own
right: you could, I imagine, find a cheap but presentable plate
on which to stand it and by writing to an alpine plant nursery as
good as the above-mentioned Ingwersen's or Broadwell Nurseries,
Moreton-in-Marsh, Gloucestershire, you can find a whole range
of lime-loving plants to bore deep into a tufa hole. Ideally you want
manageable seedlings, whose roots are not too long and whose
attached earth can be accommodated in the rock; indoors, for a
cool room which does not get much above 50°F, I would enjoy a
chunk of tufa filled with the reliable rosettes of a spring saxifrage,
preferably the lime-loving *aizoon* sort (sprays of yellow or white
flowers in April) or the furry red-stemmed *grisebachii,* especially
in its Wisley variety which has a decidedly shocking look to it.

Bolder gardeners will experiment with *Phyteuma comosum,* a
flower which I cannot really describe for you except to say that it
could be called flask-shaped, purple-flushed and black-tipped and
that it is known as one of the most glorious curiosities of an alpine
mountain; the timid will turn to a tight mat of *Sempervivums* or
houseleeks, which the Romans grew on the equally arid roofs of
their houses, thinking them to be lightning-conductors, or the

158

Saxifraga grisebachii.
6 in high, flowers March–April. Lime, sharp drainage; excellent in tufa, set vertically. Hates damp on leaves, otherwise easy. Increase by division

stonecrops *(Sedums)* which have white-coated stems and succulent leaves of purple, green or yellow according to choice. Big chunks of tufa could hold *Verbascum dumulosum,* a furry-leaved beauty with mustard-yellow flowers to a height of 9 inches, the white or blue *Campanula isophylla,* the well-known harebell of hanging baskets, or a clump of small wild pinks, especially the tight hummock of a Bulgarian one called *Dianthus simulans,* if you ever come across it.

Smaller lumps could make do very prettily with smaller campanulas, such as *raineri, zoysii, aucheri* or *pusilla,* the related forms of edraianthus, the unfailing scarlet spikes of the easy erinus, the solid small pads of *Gypsophila aretioides* or the small carpet of *Androsace sempervivoides.* Their tufa home should be watered over its surface every few days, preferably without wetting any plants with hairy leaves: it does not matter if you go away for a week and leave it dry, as the centre of tufa is porous enough to keep roots happy on the water.

For the alpines I mention you must turn down the central heating: ideally, they like protection from overhead damp and the temperature of a cold greenhouse. So do I, for heat stops me thinking: forced to choose between tufa indoors or a too high temperature, I would happily take the tufa and garden it without a need for a garden of my own.

159

The smaller the space in a garden, the better the use it must make of its time. The mention of a name like *Amelanchier canadensis* would make most gardeners shy away from it but this ordinary small tree, known as the snowy mespilus (one obscurity after another) is to my mind better value than a cherry, though it has never been popular. A cloud of small white flowers, fruits in a favourable year, then brilliant autumn colour equal to the brightest Canadian trees. Nowadays we all prefer our pink cherry trees, probably in the mistaken hope that we might one day eat their fruits. But we ought to judge a plant by its season, not only by its old associations.

This business of time can be put right only by patient and attentive study. Gardeners can consult no guide or book for the length of any one flower's season: the Swedish botanist Linnaeus did once plant a garden on the model of a clock so that a different flower would open at each hour of the day but his experiments have never been extended more usefully. Sun roses, evening primrose and that beautiful annual, the Marvel of Peru, were all part of the Swede's clock garden but none of them retains its flowers for more than two days. Back to personal observation.

There are broad differences which are as well to consider, especially when arranging a group of herbaceous plants. If you needed a true blue flower, 18 inches or 2 feet high, I suspect you would pick that rich dark Veronica called True Blue which belongs with the heaviest and most luxuriant June evening. But in a week the whole of its flower spike has dropped its petals, the lower ones falling before the top has had time to open. It leaves a boring clump of plain green for the rest of the season.

Not so the bright blue perennial flax, called *Linum narbonnense:* this is a slender spidery plant which I associate with spidery sandy gardens, but its lovely flowers keep opening for three successive months and its thin stems do sway gracefully in the wind. More value, here, than in the true blue Veronica, and if you enjoy dead-heading, the anxious gardener's best therapy, then the flax will respond to your efforts by lasting even longer.

On the further edges of the blue spectrum, the area I call nurserymen's blue, there are some conspicuous long-lasters, three of which I would not be without. Instead of the common purple border salvia, the gardener who prizes time should plant the smaller form called May Night which begins to flower in May, stops in July for dead-heading, then starts again from the axils of the leaves in August. Or he could consider a slate-blue campanula called *burghaltii*, also about two feet high and one of my past successes: this abundant and obliging plant will delight you with hanging tube-shaped flowers of its sociable colour from June till late August. Only a pale mauve-blue penstemon, pinkish in the bud and round the mouth of its tubular flowers, can outdo this: the ordinary *azureus* form lasts as long as any and responds to dead-heading from mid-May right through the summer.

The whole penstemon family, not so tender as timid gardeners suspect, should be well-represented in a long-lasting border: I could imagine an easy front grouping of a reddish penstemon called Firebird whose flowers, like all products with a name insistent on their merits, are not really as fiery as you might think, combined with the prettiest of the smaller wild geraniums called Buxton's Blue which looks its coolest and clearest in September after a summer season of interest. Very different, of course, from the bright mauve purple cranesbills of June, such as *Geranium grandiflorum,* which have nothing to promise now except the reddish autumn tints of their dying leaves, gay though this neglected feature can be.

Away from the blues and purples the long service medal must surely go to a free-flowering white viola called *cornuta alba* which is the answer to almost any gap or doubt. Its mauve form is not to my taste, but the white one, even in shade, can be left to trail between clumps of more solid favourites or even trained over a short-lived neighbour, an oriental poppy, for example, which makes such a fuss and bother with its opulent flowers for one week only, then collapses into black fly, shrivelled leaves and unforgiveable ugliness. The viola, which begins in May, will still be going strong: it has a second burst in autumn. You can cut it back, haul it up to a height of a foot or leave it flat to seed itself and multiply, though it is not an annual. Grouped near the green-flowered Corsican hellebore whose flowers will often last from January to April, it gives you a point of interest on which you can rely for most of the year. Gypsophila, Everlasting Pea and plain nasturtiums are other admirable plants for training over gaps and a dying June border. All are long-lasting flowers.

There is much more to be said, noticed and practised here, from such elementary advice as the fact that double flowers generally last longer than single flowers to the complicated effects of the weather and latitude on the season of any one flower. It seems to me, for instance, that purple and blue mauve flowers tend to last longer, perhaps because they are visited by bees, above all, for pollination. It also seems that the longest lasting flowers are not always the most beautiful, for a worthy penstemon can never compete with a bright blue and brief-lived Chilean crocus. The distinction must always be borne in mind.

One of the longest seasons, I suspect, would now be found among the most popular of the modern rose bushes. It is not unusual for Peace, Iceberg or Queen Elizabeth roses to be flowering in December, if no heavy frost has ruined their last few buds. They have begun in June and they do not demand dead-heading to keep them in flower, though it does help to keep them tidy. They do not need pruning, either, not even Peace which will make a leggy shrub of about five feet if left alone; it also flowers more freely when treated in this untidy way, for a fierce cutting back, which we give to rose bushes in the name of pruning, diverts a plant from flowering to the effort of throwing up new growth.

Amelanchier canadensis. Small tree to 20 ft, or else a medium-sized shrub. Flowers April–May. Any soil, especially lime or chalk. Fruits and bright autumn colour

These roses might, however, be outlasted by the small shrubs known as hebes. These belong in shape and requirements beneath the windows of a house in one of those narrow beds from which they will spill forwards over a path. They are evergreen, with a dully shaped leaf in the long-flowering kinds. Their shape is not attractive and becomes leggy and mean unless it is cut back hard in late spring after any frost which could kill it. The mauve and violet flowers of varieties called Margery Fish and Autumn Glory, the older and better of the two, will appear right round the year, most freely in late summer, but also in early spring and even winter if the weather is mild. A brief pruning in July encourages this winter flowering. Like a polyanthus, which shows colour in autumn, hebes bear flowers outside their main season.

They do respond to dead-heading, a slow but rewarding job as each of their seed-heads has to be picked out of the joint of the leaves and there are very many of them. Catmint, which flowers through summer and autumn, makes a vigorous and long-lasting neighbour, though it spreads forwards for a yard or more. It can be combined with the shrubby yellow potentilla, best in its clear primrose form called *arbuscula,* which is often renamed Elizabeth for the public. This shrub has a familiar season from July to October and is covered in single flowers which look like those of some large strawberry plant. Its disadvantage is its dead and twiggy appearance in winter, too lifeless for me to want it near the house where it is usually planted; if you break a branch in winter, do not be misled by its brown and apparently lifeless pith. That is quite normal, though it would be a sign of death in most other plants. Avoid the orange and tangerine novelties, as they are hideous. The white is often small-flowered and disappointing.

Resisting the call of long-lasting border plants, such as the white campanula called *alliariaefolia*, some 2 feet high, or the white, violet and rose flowered tradescantias with their amusingly disordered leaves, I return to what I propose to be the longest-flowering shrub in the English garden.

'God gave us memories that we might have roses in December': the first conclusion to draw from that remark is that J. M. Barrie had never grown China roses in his garden. For you do not need an all-embracing memory or a quiet half-hour in which to think back over the high garden moments of summer in order to enjoy a China rose in the depths of winter.

The thought would have horrified those ancient Roman philosophers who condemned the taste for forcing roses into flower in winter as an extreme example of perverting nature in the interests of luxury. But in the Romans' day, China roses were not widely grown: I read that the earliest known occurrence of a China rose in the west is in a corner of a Bronzino picture, and that, of course, is centuries after the Roman Empire.

Any winter flower is obviously vulnerable; you can watch the tips of your January irises piercing their way through the earth and then find that a fortnight of deep snow destroys their

Campanula alliariaefolia. Up to 2 ft, herbaceous. Tolerates dry shade, any dry soil. Flowers July onwards. Very easy from seed or divisions

blue flowers just as they begin to unfold. But a China rose is more robust than most other winter-flowering shrubs, especially if you choose the right variety and agree with me that winter begins in execrable November. As soon as you see buds on any rose late in the year, you should cut them with some colour showing and bring them indoors where the heating will speed them along remarkably well. But even if you miss your chance with the scissors, a China rose may still surprise you by opening full and wide outdoors to a show of pink among your otherwise moribund borders.

The most persistent flowerer is a variety which I have never grown myself but those who know *Rosa mutabilis* tell me that it can be relied upon to produce some colour even in early December. Its name means the 'changeable rose' and it deserves the title by bearing buds of flame-orange which pass in due order from apricot to pink to near-crimson as they age; its shape is rather thin and upright but its leaves are a good dark green. It begins its season in May and though it is never spectacular, it is always worth a visit right through the year. When I have a corner which needs a graceful filling without too much dazzling colour, I will give this chameleon-like rose bush a chance.

But the variety which I particularly urge you to try is rather more conventional. Its name is Natalie Nypels, not a lady, I feel, whom I would ever have wanted to meet. But its merits more than compensate. I had never grown it until four years ago and it was one of our garden's successes in 1970. Its shape is not very inspiring, for it makes a typical twiggy rose bush about two feet high. If it were used as a mass bedding plant, it would certainly become rather boring. But its semi-double pink flowers refuse to give up, whatever the weather.

Its first burst came in early June and even in late July, that awkward moment when all old roses are hanging fire, its small shape was alive with shell-pink clusters of its 2-inch wide flowers. We had planted half a dozen in the light shade of a walnut tree and half a dozen in a sunny new bed, and between them they kept the whole summer alive and were still in bud in the first week of December. The sunny ones flowered first, the shady ones a week later and this carefully planned show continued unabated. Mixed with silver cotton lavender or casually scattered amongst a bed of hostas with a backing of grey-leaved buddleia and some plants of dark-leaved fennel for contrast, they would give a perpetual touch of interest and would bring the various shades of their neighbours' leaves to life.

Natalie Nypels is definitely a lady to be concealed among the charms of others, but she is none the worse for that. I prefer her to the China rose which most people know: Cecil Brunner, with its tiny double flowers of the most delicate shell-pink. It is certainly more subtle but I find it a little too reminiscent of those monstrous miniature roses which tend to appear at summer flower shows. The climbing Cecile Brunner I find a very different matter,

a very original plant which will one day climb all over a 20-foot wall and reward you with clusters of small China flowers. I would like to see it against a wall of warm, grey stone: in a sheltered corner it flowers from May until late October, though I have even seen a flower or two lurking at the top as late as the beginning of December.

If I had to choose a smaller companion for Natalie, it would, I think, be *Rosa hermosa,* a China variety with pleasing grey leaves and a 3-foot-high slender shape. It too is rose-pink and lasts well into winter. But you must not expect perfectly shaped flowers though they do deserve the name of double.

With any of these varieties you can prolong the season of your garden and in a small, modern space there is nothing more important. Their winter behaviour is not a freak chance – unlike that of the hybrid teas, some of whom do sometimes last very late indeed. With these pink roses, you can even hope for a rose at Christmas, weather permitting – not, I grant you, like the Spotless Rose of the carols sprung from the Rod of Jesse, but instead born on a low, prickly bush which was given to the western world rather less dramatically by a gradual escape from behind the Wall of China.

Until this year I had never believed that Father Christmas was sympathetic to mistakes. There have been times when meaning to be given one book, I have asked by mistake for a near equivalent; the equivalent has always been the result. I once asked for a trowel and got a bath-towel, because I did not write my request out clearly enough; I sent a plain message up the chimney this time, and when, at the third attempt, it finally spiralled upwards instead of floating downwards, I felt confident of being given what I wanted: I had asked for an amaryllis.

Fortunately, the old boy knew enough botany to see what I meant. The only amaryllis with which gardeners are familiar is a pretty pink-flowered bulb called *Amaryllis belladonna.* This can be grown outdoors if you happen to live in a warm area with a narrow flowerbed beneath the south wall of your house. Then, this South African native can be planted with its neck poking out of the ground and, if the spring and summer are sunny, it will oblige with its trumpet-shaped flowers in early September. The stems stand 2 feet tall, naked when in flower and somehow too indecent for my garden. I prefer its cousin, the Nerine or Guernsey lily. Yet I asked for amaryllis and had no right to expect anything else.

What I meant, however, was a much more luxurious bulb called hippeastrum. This is a startling winter house plant which often turns up, looking most incongruous, in other people's drawing rooms, balancing in a large and unconcealable clay pot. When you ask what it is, the owner always calls it amaryllis: it sounds more romantic that way, 'sporting with amaryllis in the shade', rather than with a hippeastrum, which suggests, if anything, a drop-out American millionaire. The two flowers look very similar, though a hippeastrum would never put up with an English winter

Rose *Chinensis* 'Old Blush', China Rose. Any soil, long flowering, from June onwards. Easy from summer or autumn cuttings, the former being quicker. Up to 5 ft

outdoors. But whereas a true amaryllis would have to be concealed among my winter irises, who would resent it, I could usefully fit a hippeastrum into the front hall, where it would brighten up the early spring months.

After my muddled request I am now the happy owner of two hippeastrums from a chain store, complete with a plastic pot (in my opinion, too small) and a polythene bag full of compost and artificial fertilizer. It is time to be planting at once. Like horses and children, hippeastrums enjoy a routine. As long as you do not plant them outside, there is no problem about coaxing them into flower; they would even succeed in a saucer on a windowsill, without any soil or potting. But they would not be prepared to stand such treatment for two consecutive seasons as they would have no means of building up strength on a windowsill with which to feed their flower-bud for the following year.

One of the first lessons to be learnt by a keen bulb-grower is that the months after flowering are vitally important. Bulbs do not merely need a few weeks' attention when in bud; you cannot expect to divide their dormant clumps in late summer if you only give them a handful of that over-rated fertilizer, bonemeal, when you have nothing better to do in February. The moment to be giving them most affection is when they are in leaf. With hippeastrums, the importance of leaves is especially obvious.

They usually flower stark naked, except for a modestly emerging pair of sword-shaped leaves at the base; you have to put up with a 2-foot stem, stiffly upright, topped by three, four or (very rarely) five flowers which are shaped like wide open funnels and could be

Amaryllis belladonna, true Amaryllis. Up to 3 ft, outdoors in sunniest possible bed against a wall. Do not bury the bulb, and feed well after flowering

mistaken for lilies if they were not of such a thick texture. Thanks to the enterprise of large chain-stores you can have them in dark red, pink, white, or pink and white stripes as supplied by Dutch growers. Though often disturbed by the cut-price offers, allegedly of quality, which deceive so many gardeners in the press or supermarkets, I see no guile in these packaged hippeastrums and I warmly recommend them, even to owners of a town flat.

You pot them up either in the accompanying compost or in your garden soil, provided it is not sticky clay or acid and waterlogged bog. You then leave them in their pot, 5- or 6-inches in diameter, in a warm and light spot inside your house. It is fun to watch their sudden and rapid progress, so they make an entertaining addition to the downstairs décor. All you need to do is to keep them watered every other day; no matter if you go away for a weekend and have to neglect them. Their flowering-date depends on your central heating and your planting season.

As I agree with alpine plants and like to be cold, those I plant in late December will probably not be flowering before mid-March. But if you begin watering and planting in October in a warm room, you would certainly have a hippeastrum in flower for Christmas.

After flowering you must be alert and persistent. The bulb sends up long and floppy green leaves which respond to daily watering and fortnightly feeding with liquid manure. Only in August do these lush and troublesome leaves begin to wither. At once, stop watering and allow them to die away, so that they can be cut off and the bulb can be repotted in fresh compost for the following year. As a result of all this after-care, you will have built up a well-fed bud for next spring and you will find that your parent bulb begins to produce contented children beside it which can be split up and grown on or given away. But if you lose interest once your bulb has flowered, it will never be so beautiful again.

The hippeastrum begs you to look after it: you decide when to begin giving it light and water; it rewards you with prompt flower and growth. You stop watering; within weeks it will die down. It is cumbersome when out of flower and, being tall and naked, it is not easy to place in a house. It looks best when stood in a passage or hall. But it is obligingly exotic and I urge you to give it the routine it needs. It seems so paradoxical that what began as a Christmas parcel will end, within ten weeks, over 2 feet tall and the envy of all who see it.

Presumably, every reader has an ambition which has yet to be realised; the trouble with mine, I told myself last spring, was that I had devoted so much time, money and energy to it, and it was not really very ambitious after all. I just wanted to see masses of garden-worthy wild flowers growing in nature; I do, however, stress the garden-worthy, as so often field botanists lose their hearts to sandworts or rare sedge grasses which may be thrilling as lost links in the earth's evolution but which, to a gardener's eye, are about as appealing as a field of groundsel.

No, I wanted lilies, narcissus, roses and at least two million

Hippeastrum, the so-called Amaryllis. A bulb, it can be forced for winter. Remember to water and feed well after flowering; then its children can be detached and grown separately

primroses: I tried Switzerland, but arrived when the cows had already cropped the lower pastures, and I found that I had headaches at heights. I tried Bavaria, on an expedition to see the Lady's Slipper orchid, and after two days' walk with a team of ladies in *lederhosen* we did indeed find it, but only in seed, and I was sitting on it.

I went to Greece but was diverted, regrettably, by the ruins. It was made worse by my belonging to a society whose quarterly bulletin was filled with other members' happy holidays. There were maps of where to walk for cyclamen in Yugoslavia, there were arguments about whether the Hon. Secretary had found *Iris histrioides* or *histrioides major* growing by the thousand in the Balkans.

So when, in 1972, I was going to travel in the Arctic Ocean, aboard a canoe made of walrus-skin, I packed warm trousers, vitamin pills and water-wings, and only as an afterthought included my trowel and a collection of polythene bags. What, after all, could possibly grow in a summer of two months and a winter of –50°F? The answer, apart from a billion mosquitoes, was almost everything I could have wished to see. If the life of the sea multiplies the nearer man goes to the North Pole, the same, from my point of view, could be said of the life of the mountains. Space seems infinite, as the icepack stretches away to the sea's horizon, and time seems frantically quickened, as snow melts in a week, willows and tundra appear beneath and a host of plants flower, fade and set seed in the course of summer's six weeks or so.

In three months I saw the full cycle of the seasons, winter mercifully excepted. The salmonberries and other relations of the rubus whose pink and white bramble flowers I had admired in July were bearing their berries by mid-August and turning their leaves to reds and purples within another week. The first time I saw a hillside of arctic poppies I thought I would return and photograph them a week later; when I came back, they were already setting seed, knowing they must hurry through the few days which served as summer. At last, not even I could miss. Spring, summer and autumn were happening everywhere at once, and the abundance startled me after so many failed visits to find it.

The richest sites lie either inside the Brooks range of mountains or else on the edge of the Arctic Circle, on the western coast of Alaska, where the conditions of marsh, moor, seashore and mountain cliff-face can often be seen in succession in a walk of only an hour. On one such walk I moved from blue marsh irises and bog myrtle to a scrub of Arctic willow, then up to carpets of our native dryas, oak leaved and white flowered, mixed with dodecatheon, or shooting stars, five different kinds of poppy, pink silene or campion, a beautiful crucifer called *Parrya* after a British admiral, three potentillas, so much *Anemone sylvestris* that I trampled on it without any scruples. Arctic forget-me-not and three different colours of lousewort, so much more beautiful than its name.

I was then, after half an hour, within sight of the seashore, home of fourteen wild Eskimo vegetables, true blue mertensia and a purple cousin of our own sweet pea, and above me rose an alpine

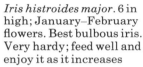

Iris histroides major. 6 in high; January–February flowers. Best bulbous iris. Very hardy; feed well and enjoy it as it increases

scree, covered, to my amazement, with white brothers of the androsaces that climbers risk their necks to see in the Alps, grey-white gentians, brilliant scarlet anemone, violet harebells, two cushion saxifrages and the cousin of the King of the Alps itself, the legendary eritrichium, here in its rare *aretioides* form, 2 inches high and 3 inches wide, but so blue that few cameras ever capture it and so fussy and hairy that no gardener has ever grown it properly despite a thousand attempts at collection. Rewarded at last, in the least likely landscape, I sat down among delphiniums, a fumitory and a glacial buttercup and tried to beat away the mosquitoes which I had not learnt to leave alone.

Manure and water, never forget it, are the gardener's best friends, and not only in the vegetable garden, either, for it is a biased and human view that beauties are better if they do not eat or drink. The Arctic points this lesson clearly. Where melted snow runs down the hillsides, the rare Bering Strait primrose, *Primula beringensis*, grows in abundance, showing a mass of the small rose-coloured flowers which know no other home in the world. In similar rockfaces 20 yards away there is no trickling water, and so no primroses.

The same applies to manure. Where the dogteams of huskies are chained for the summer, greeting each change in the wind with a howl, there are clumps of the best yellow poppy, *Papaver radicatum*, mixed with mats of dark blue forget-me-nots or *Myosotis alpestris*. Who would have thought that the poppy would be the symbol of summer in the Arctic circle? Here, the reason for its special luxuriance lies with the dog teams: they manured it, and I never saw it so richly coloured again.

Upon the hills, it is a sparser and more alpine world; here the snow still lies in places as a blanket. Prospective owners of alpine plants and gardens are always advised to see mountain flowers in the wild in order to appreciate what is needed. Very sharp drainage through chipped stone and desert-dry peat, plenty of water from melting snow, intense and clear light; these are what an Arctic mountain can offer, and it is no wonder that alpine gardeners in England have such a hard time of it.

There, four of the Arctic's many saxifrages grew in tightest hummocks, none the worse for soil only 2 inches deep and winter frosts which snows can only lessen, not keep off. I am extremely fond of the rock jasmines, or androsaces, which range from the coarse and leafy to the hairiest and fussiest small tussocks, and here there were clumps of a small pink variety called *ochetensis*, again unknown elsewhere, which had hidden themselves in a mass of flowers, like one mop-headed chrysanthemum.

But it was the tundra that intrigued me most, for travelling along the north of America to the Northwest Passage, down a route which had seen 300 whaling boats to their doom in the past hundred years, I came to know its every peculiarity, like some old and exotic friend. There were days when we would have ridden the sea's swell all night and would turn at last to the shore to

Nerine undulatifolia, Guernsey Lily. 2 ft high; flowers September–October. Best below a sunny wall, only covered up to neck of the bulb

170

Above: *Saxifraga hypnoides* and *Meconopsis cambrica,* wild Saxifraga and Welsh Poppy in April

Below: *Eritrichium nanum,* King of the Alps, in the Alpine Section of the Munich Botanical Gardens. Men have risked their necks on climbing ropes to see this purest of all blue flowers. Its hairy leaf makes it almost impossible to grow out-doors in Great Britain, so please do not collect it if you find yourself dangling in front of it

Left: *Papaver radicatum* in the Schachengarten, Bavaria: the world's finest rock garden, actually set on a high mountainside, only accessible on foot. Worth the walk in July

View of tundra in July, flanking the North-West passage. Note the regimented ponds and be thankful for the absence of their regimented mosquitoes

beach and dry out our skins, both human and walrus, for the boat-skins, too, grew soft with use.

We would climb an unnamed beach-ridge and run to keep warm on a tundra landscape which no one, perhaps, had visited before us. Tundra (the word means 'without trees') is damp, dark and spongy, like elemental peat, and at a depth of 2 feet or less it rests on permanent frost. It never, therefore, drains, and is covered in pools of melted ice, which show up as blue as a kingfisher under the twenty-four hours of sunlight that make up most summer days. As if by some primeval conspiracy, every tundra pond lies on the same axis, facing northeast and southwest, perhaps because of winter's prevailing wind.

We would jump and stamp to bring back the blood to our legs, and our Eskimos would bring driftwood, the natural rubbish of the Arctic, with which we would settle down to make the fire. There would be white cotton-grass and clear yellow poppy, half a dozen of the Arctic's fifty saxifrages, buttercups wedged between blocks of tundra, lichens and mosses whose links lay often with those of New Zealand and thus were a possible echo of the ecology of twenty million years ago.

My ambition had been realized when I almost despaired of it; the sun would light up the sedge-browns and moss-greens of Herschel Island, and I would enjoy it the more for knowing that others could hardly choose to come and see it too. And now, there are pavements all over poor old England; my neighbours only come down for weekends; there is talk of street-lighting to bring the village up to date. I have seen garden flowers in the wild, as I wanted, and yet I am not quite sure that by seeing the wild, I have not also changed my beliefs in what a garden could offer and how an English garden should be.

174

The Wild Garden

Wild gardening sounds as attractive nowadays as a wild woman or a wild party. Those patient hours of seed-raising, hoeing and spraying can be abandoned in a wild garden. Nature, so the theory goes, will do the work in a wood or orchard which would otherwise prove too much for its owner. We are all being tempted by the wilderness, believing that its ground can be covered with one of those ground-covering creepers and that the devil can then be left to do his worst on a mere three days' work a month.

I was trying recently to tempt a group of gardeners with rare alpine plants and the raising of other countries' wild flowers from seed. Their interest only revived with the mention of wild flowers. When I referred to wild gardening on the way through, up went a hand or two to ask if I could be more explicit. As an idea a wild garden sounds lazy and romantic. Like all romances, it is better explored before you take it too far.

Wild gardening is difficult, its beauty elusive and never achieved without planned effort. For the gardener who wants a reliable show in a wild piece of field or former kitchen garden adjoining his own I can recommend nothing more strongly than bulbs. This may sound dull because we all know that bulbs can be naturalized, yet they are the only form of lazy wild gardening which is always satisfactory. The most frequent error is an excessive keenness to tidy them up.

Ideally, the long grass in which bulbs are planted should not be cut before late June so that the bulbs can seed themselves and die down with fully ripened leaves. The cutting is not easy, and conventional rotary mowers of my acquaintance will soon seize up in serious long grass. Do not despise the familiar scythe, though left-handers like myself find it awkward. It cuts more quickly and easily than machine-sellers ever admit and it is as due for a revival as old barbers' razors and their leather strops.

The modern version called the Swing-King cutter is not entirely useless, though I cannot say it cuts a swathe through grass which has been left to grow till July. The rich man will prefer the grand Allen scythes, motor-powered, solid, two-wheeled and unbeatable among any hay croppers. They are heavy to turn and control until you are used to them and will damage any tree whose trunk is bumped by their double row of fangs. But they do cut 2-foot-high grass and cow-parsley in late June and August. Lower grass is best handled by the reliable mowers in the Mountfield range.

If bulbs sound ordinary, ask yourself whether you have tried to naturalize wild anemones, Stars of Bethlehem, Snake's Head fritillaries, Lent lilies, ornamental onion or autumn crocus. I would guess that you have not. Of these, the forms of *Anemone blanda* are beyond reproach. They are cheap, especially in their mixture of rose, white and pale violet which is the prettiest combination. They spread rapidly, especially in light soil. They flower abundantly, and even if they only open their flowers to their full width of an inch and a half in bright light, they flower in March and April when sunny periods are likely. They are 3 inches

high and matched with a sea-green leaf, cut into a delicate shape.

Their red relations called *Anemone pavonina*, the peacock anemone, are possibly even more lovely, but they are happier in an open and sunny bed where they do not compete with turf. I cannot imagine why these anemones are not popular. I promise those of you who are as bored with the florists' St Brigid anemones as I am that these two sorts, *blanda* and *pavonina*, are wild wind-flowers, graceful, simple and wise enough not to flower the whole year round for the stock of every barrow-boy.

Wild windflowers, then, for a wild bulb-garden, and perhaps with clumps of the uncommon wild gladiolus called *byzantinus* to add interest in late summer. I marked this down from the flora of the Mediterranean as a bulb for my next orchard. Its spikes of magenta-purple flowers are slender and elegant, quite unlike the florists' autumn gladioli. It grows in French cornfields and likes a sunny home. It is not expensive.

The autumn crocus would be an obvious successor to the second grass-cut in the wild garden's year. It is possible to cut down an orchard in late August without ruining the snouts of a late crocus like *zonatus* which is just showing through the ground. The common *speciosus* is a prettier shade of pale violet, but it begins to grow earlier and is likely to be damaged during this late summer mowing. Other autumn crocuses are lovely and often sweetly scented, but I prefer them in pots or in a raised bed, perhaps on top of a small wall, where they can be admired more closely.

Back in the spring the finest daffodil for wild gardening, to my eye, is the smallest, our own wild Lent lily (*Narcissus pseudo-narcissus*) which is pale lemon and primrose and only 6 inches high. This, an English wild flower, is so much more natural than a drift of golden-yellow giant trumpets. If you want a bright yellow try the Tenby daffodil (*Narcissus obvallaris*) another English native and only 9 inches high. Spring bulbs in a wild garden should look like the foreground of a Botticelli painting where they stud the ground in single pinks and whites. They should not be massed in 2-foot-high bunches as if on a stall in Covent Garden.

Gardeners near bluebell woods need look no further for their wild garden's bulbs. The white varieties of the false bluebell, *Scilla campanulata*, also match those drifts of firm blue most pleasingly. The sensible gardener will always look at his local wild flowers before planting his own wild garden. Those who are denied the charm of bluebells locally, perhaps because their garden is too open and sunny, can content themselves with the small white and green flowered Star of Bethlehem (*Ornithogalum umbellatum*) and a rampant wild white garlic called *Allium ursinum*. These are vigorous and never out of place.

A good wild garden should be built in layers, from wild bulbs up to suitable shrubs and trees. I must now climb up a layer to herbaceous plants where the wilderness's problems begin. But the first step is to recognize the bulbs, look for wild forms for a true wild garden and realize that bulbs will flower in summer and

Anemone blanda. Grows up to 4 in, flowers in April, opens petals in sunlight. Rampant on light soils. Worth scattering its own seed round it. Grow from bafflingly wrinkled corms; I have never yet lost them whichever way up I have planted them

177

autumn and that there is more to an orchard than half a hundred-weight of butter-yellow daffodils.

Wild gardening above bulbs will only work if it is planned in layers. Smug books on gardening like to tell their readers to watch and follow Nature as their final authority. The fashion for eco-gardens with micro-zones of inter-structured nature seems to me to be a worthless way of stating the same problems differently, yet I would urge the owner of a possible wild garden who has planted bulbs to look next at a nearby copse or former railway embankment and wonder why he loves it. By loving a stretch of nature, he will be ready to return and plant one of the few successful wild gardens to have been laid out. There is much talk of wild gardening, but I have yet to see a satisfactory one which gardens without becoming tame.

The man who begins by observing a bank or a wood will not mix rhododendrons and hybrid azaleas, plant them in limestone landscapes nor, preferably, plant them in masses at all. Massed rhododendrons are a race apart, as distinct as priests from their audience. They have their own stud books, and in the grandest gardens they live in fenced enclosures like a herd in a dangerous zoo. Cornwall and Scotland are the landscapes where they look most natural, but they have taken over Surrey, a bit of Berkshire and too much else. I like a few of them as individuals, but the larger ones depress me in a wild English setting. A planting of mixed azaleas, and azaleas only, can look tolerably wild, especially if the whites are kept back in the darkest shade and the reds, pinks and yellows are graded in bands into each other, like the many colours in a fire. Unlike most rhododendrons, azaleas do not block the light with solid and unpolished evergreen leaves.

The observer of nature will do better to take his wild garden from the hints of his own wild flowers. Where English ditches have cranesbill and cow-parsley he will allow himself their improved relations, *Geranium macrorrhizum* or the selected white and pale blue forms of *pratense* and *sylvaticum*. His cow-parsley will be the larger and finer-leaved *Selinum tenuifolium*. Among anemones, he may choose the rampageous form called *vitifolia* which has run wild in hedgerows in southern Ireland and produces the same single rose-pink flowers as the Japanese kinds in the garden. This is smaller-flowered, but very much quicker to take hold. The form called *robustissima* speaks for itself.

Smaller herbaceous flowering plants are the most difficult layer to maintain and enjoy. These smaller plants must compete with weeds and long grass, as all beds and formal borders kill the idea of wild gardening. They can only be bedded, in my opinion, if they are massed in a very few varieties in order to cover the ground completely, as if your wood has been visited by some new but plausible weed.

I do stress the need for only a few varieties; if you disagree, spend a summer afternoon in the lower slopes of the National Trust's garden at Hidcote in Gloucestershire where the range of

Above: *Geranium macrorrhizum album*. White Cranesbill, up to a foot, very spreading. Any soil, even dry shade. Flowers June–July. The best way to smother woodland weeds, if planted in clean soil

Below: *Selinum tenuifolium*, cow parsley in improved garden form. 4–5 ft; June flowering. Architectural. Likes rich soil, happy in shade. Do not despise it

ground-cover is exhausting to the eye. At the end, you should ask
yourself whether it would not have been far prettier with rough
grass and the wild flowers of an English field. So fine is the bound-
ary between wild and fussy gardening.

The plausible weeds I have mentioned would again be related
to our own flora. Before massing them, the ground must be
thoroughly cleared, and seen to be clear for at least three months.
This means persistent attack with a strong selective weedkiller,
probably a brushwood killer like the effective SBK, followed by
any of the many brands (Weedol and so forth) which kill annual
weeds, either by poisoning the ground against their seeds or else
by acting through their leaves. There is no quick way to kill an
adult dock, though two years' barrage with any brand containing
the compound called mecocrop will usually bring it to surrender.
The poisoning of future wild gardens has to be timed to suit their

established weeds. Annual weeds can be treated effectively through the soil in spring before they germinate, but a perennial beauty like bindweed must be attacked when it is in leaf. So, too, with ground elder. The poisoner's calender is a full one, and my advice to any wild gardener is to set aside a whole season from spring to autumn in order to kill before he plants.

Only when nettles and bindweed are out of the earth can he replace them with his chosen wild covering. This must be rampant, tidy and simple-flowered, such as might be found on the floor of a nearby forest. Books recommend hostas and bergenias, that invariable pair for mass landscaping. Both look unnatural, tame and about as plausible as a leopard in a beech wood. I would suggest, instead, a broad-leaved and particularly rampant form of the wild woodrush, called *Luzula maxima sylvatica*. This is appallingly greedy and very quick to grow. It forms a thicket of rushy green leaves and is the answer to dry shade under trees, sloping banks or wild areas which cannot be controlled by mowing. Although it is too tough a layer for most bulbs, it will combine with woodland shrubs, none more suitable than the improved forms of our wild snowberry *(Symphoricarpos)*, especially Hancocks variety with its strings of pink-white berries in winter.

Periwinkle would please those who are scared of the woodrush or cannot contain it. *Vinca minor* is the one obliging form, so avoid the slower and larger *major*. Avoid too the variegated kinds, pretty though they are, for they are too stylish to belong in a wild or woodland setting. That is the wild gardener's problem. He must choose plants with a wild feel about them and resist all artificiality, more beautiful though it may seem in isolation. A wilderness must never be spotted with too many varieties, each exampled in too few plants. It must not be cut up in beds or filled with the plants of a formal garden, with roses like Queen Elizabeth, perennials like the rose-red sedum or the summer phlox, with too many double flowers, dahlias or chrysanthemums of any kind.

Exclude any plant which cannot cover the ground cleared for it or which cannot survive among such rampant substitutes for weeds. Grand books on gardening recommend lilies and the stately cardiocrinum as bulbs for wild woodland. Gardeners on acid soil may be able to make lilies at home in quantity, but only by planting them in recognized clearings where they look lovely, but in no sense wild. The martagon lily, especially in its white form, is to my eye the nearest a lily can come to looking wild and natural in England. Groups of *auratum* lilies do look and smell magnificent but they are exactly wrong for what I see as a proper wild garden.

The same goes for polyanthus. It was Miss Jekyll who first had the idea of massing forms of primrose under hazelnut trees. The seed of the bunch-flowered yellow varieties which she collected for forty years is still marketed by Thompson and Morgan, London Road, Ipswich. Like many of her ideas, it was taken up at Sissinghurst Castle where a wonderful carpet of polyanthus of all

An excellent example of wild planting in a natural landscape too bold for normal gardening: St Colombs, Co. Donegal, Eire, garden of Derek Hill

colours can be admired each spring.

Yet the division, weeding and replacement of these polyanthus is a long labour not to be undertaken in a wild garden away from the civilized cover of nut trees. The mixed polyanthus, especially, would look too formal to be credible, and credibility is the test of a planted wilderness. If primroses will spread naturally in your garden, by all means leave them to thicken into a carpet of their one pale shade of yellow. But do not bed them out deliberately, each in the implausible colours of the polyanthus varieties.

The wild garden's perennials should surely be close to our own wild flowers. I keep stressing this and in support I ask you to think of the foxglove, perhaps most handsome when grown from seed of the strawberry-coloured form called *mertonensis*. This plant can be enjoyed in West Country hedgerows and looks elegant in any wild setting where its basal clump of leaves is too lowly and tough to be upset by summer mowing. Incidentally, growers of foxgloves need never be short of house plants, for a foxglove can be lifted when in bud, potted up from the open ground and kept quite content until its gloves drop in due season. If you do not fancy the idea of tall foxgloves indoors, try massing them in a hall or passage where they will stand out like a group of spires.

The same development of our native wildness can be followed through the hellebore, the cranesbill, the fumitory, sweet wood-ruff, comfrey, wild iris and the shrubby rubuses, relations of our wild bramble. I can imagine a plausible wild garden planted solely with forms of these wild flowers, and nothing else except bulbs.

The hellebore would be the green-flowered *foetidus*, whose thin and glossy leaves are well able to cope with a surrounding carpet of ground-cover. The cranesbill would weave such a carpet with selected forms of its meadow-varieties (*Geranium pratense*) which seed so freely. They could be underplanted with the large mats and running clumps of forms like *macrorrhizum, nodosum* and *grandiflorum*. There is no apter plant for the wild garden than a cranesbill.

The fumitories are more delicate and would have to be placed in carefully cleared patches on the edge of the rampant tangle. All forms of fumitory are worth collecting, especially the pale-cream-flowered *Corydalis ochroleuca*, and they soon start seeding themselves. Sweet woodruff (*Asperula odorata*) is small and lowly but will also smother a shaded clearing, especially if the earth is damp, a taste shared by the fumitories which match it neatly. Its white flowers smell of mown hay. Tiny though they are, they are too delicious to neglect.

The comfrey is coarser but an admirable blue, as I found when we massed it near the white *Azalea palestrina* for one of the *Financial Times*'s gardens at the Chelsea Flower Show. It is coarse-leaved and pinkish on the outside of its buds in the manner of the borage family. It will compete with dry shade and weeds and is not upset by a scything or mowing which removes its ragged

Symphytum grandiflorum, Wild Comfrey. Up to 3 ft; May–June flowering. Any soil or dry shade. Pull off leaves if they look messy. Easy from seed or division; blue, tipped with pink

Euonymus alatus (in foreground) at Westonbirt, form of Spindle Tree. Will grow on lime; slow to height of 10 ft. Excellent autumn colour

summer leaves. Like the perennial forget-me-not, *Brunnera macrophylla*, the comfreys are excellent wild plants until early June. The common form, *Symphytum grandiflorum*, is as good as any, growing about two feet tall and flowering freely. *Caucasicum* is more delicate but *peregrinum* is also worth a place in a wilderness. The rubus before which they could be grouped would be the rampant and magnificent *Rubus cockburnianus* whose tangle of white-washed stems is unmistakably pretty in winter. It is almost worth having a wild garden in order to grow this relation of the bramble. From November on it looks as if it had been sprayed with white paint and fits excellently into a wild setting. The evergreen *Rubus tricolor* is a low-growing creeper which also cannot be ignored. There is no faster plant to cover a wide space of bare earth. Its rounded leaves are a glossy evergreen and its trailing stems will often extend 4 yards in a year. But they do become involved in each other and surge up into a tangle as much as 2 feet high. This does not matter in the background of a wilderness and although this rubus does not flower it is the quickest return that the wild gardener can enjoy. Being a relation of our wild bramble, though not so prickly, its hairy stems do not look inappropriate in an English woodland or orchard.

Above the bulbs, the creepers and the small shrubs, the wild gardener needs drifts and thickets of leaves and bushes, wild enough to compete with the layers beneath them and not so formal that they ruin the plausible wilderness in which they are meant to be growing. Gardeners on acid soils will continue to reach for their rhododendrons, whatever I write here, but I do wish we used more skimmias, those fresh-leaved evergreens with sweet white flowers and red berries, if male and female stand near each other. They have a lightness of leaf and a compact firmness of outline which matches well with an English wood or open heath.

I also commend the blueberry to wild gardeners in Scotland and similar areas. This likes a damp, shaded home where the biggest, called *corymbosum*, will grow at least 5 feet high and wide and bear those blue autumn berries, so delicious when mixed with wild fraises des bois, before the leaves go red and fall. Our native bilberry is lower and humbler, called *myrtillus:* the evergreen *myrsinites* reaches 3 feet eventually and is an equally useful wild shrub for background throughout the year. Again the wild garden will look most convincing when planted with forms of our own naturalized flora. I do not pretend that a blueberry is as beautiful as a camellia, but it does look less stylized.

There are a few more appropriate sights than autumn colour in a wild or woodland garden. The flaming reds and yellows can be banked down the sides of a path through a wood or orchard; there, like a fresh lime-green in spring, they are shown off most clearly by the light that falls on them through the trees above. A well-spaced plantation of larch trees, so seldom recommended in this age of solid conifers, forms a fine roof for these autumn colours, while larch needles are a useful blanket, once fallen, against weeds. Of course, these autumn colours would look charming against the trunks of birch trees, but birch and beech are not easily underplanted, because of their root systems. Avoid plane trees, too, if only because their leaves take several seasons to rot down into compost.

Among blueberries in autumn I would willingly mass our native spindle tree, controllable to a height of 5 or 6 feet if bought in bush form as plain *Euonymus alatus*. This interestingly shaped bush will grow in any semi-shaded wood, liking lime too. Its blazing autumn colour is magnificent, especially when planted generously. It seeds itself with the help of its winged seeds.

I would of course combine it, given space, with those favourites which always preoccupy me in autumn: dogwood in its bright red Westonbirt form, its yellow one and even its plum one (though remember that the pretty variegated kind is less vigorous), and the scarlet and egg-yellow winter twigs of the smaller willows *(Salix chermesina* and others), kept pruned as shrubs.

The further this wild garden goes, the more it trades on forms related to our native flora. Of course much of this flora may not be indigenous but it has only flourished here since its introduction because its new home felt, and usually looked, appropriate. By urging you to try out Guelder rose in the wild garden I am drawing on the same stock. This tough native shrub is seldom dull, bearing those lovely greenish-white heads of flower in May and clusters of shiny rose-red berries in autumn. A fine form is sold by Notcutt's, Woodbridge, Suffolk, as Notcutt's Variety of *Viburnum opulus*. The Guelder rose, as Miss Jekyll first discovered, will thrive in more shade than catalogues suggest. She grouped it under a white *Clematis montana* on a north wall, a combination which flowered in similar colours at a similar season and which would be worth imitating.

The wider-spreading *Viburnum tomentosum,* especially in forms such as Lanarth, would cover more ground more dramatically. Its branches spread horizontally and its white flowers are born on slender stems. It will thrive in a wild garden, but it is slow-growing if kept too shaded. It does enjoy lime or even chalk. Allow it plenty of space.

Rather than combine these deciduous shrubs with a horizontal evergreen, the cotoneaster or the useful horizontal 'laurel' *Prunus* Otto Luykens, I would rely on holly for a glossy leaf of lasting green. It grows slowly, I know, but so often it can be found lingering under tall trees, where few books imply it would be happy. Laurel and cotoneaster are useful, sometimes even attractive in screen plantings near a house. But they are too drab and formal for a wild garden. Give me a sweep of holly instead, as long as I did not have to weed by hand among its prickly fall-out. Holly, I need hardly add, has naturalized itself in England, whereas other evergreen, except box and bush ivy, have not. Wild gardening should begin and end with hints from our own English wilderness. It is only the gardener who has inherited the rude idea of weeds.

Index

The publishers would like to thank the following for permission to reproduce their photographs:

Pat Brindley: 14, 20, 28, 29, 30, 32, 41, 42, 57, 80, 88, 97, 98, 99, 102, 107, 118, 119, 120, 136, 146, 151, 164, 179, 180, 186; Valerie Finnis: frontispiece, 12, 17, 18, 21, 22, 24, 35, 36, 42, 43, 46, 49, 59, 62, 63, 68, 72, 76, 81, 84, 93, 94, 104, 111, 112, 115, 120, 122, 141, 144, 148, 152, 155, 156, 157, 161, 171, 172, 182, 183; Derek Hill: 184; Anthony Huxley: 40, 47, 90, 128, 166, 169, 181; Harold Langford, A.R.P.S.: half-title, title, 10, 14, 16, 19, 20, 23, 25, 26, 34, 35, 45, 47, 56, 62, 63, 64, 71, 82/3, 97, 105, 108, 112, 122/3, 124, 133, 134, 135, 141, 142/3, 153, 154, 158, 168, 176, 182, 187; Michael R. L. Astor: 174; The National Trust: 94; The Schacht Collection: 173.